THE PRACTICE
OF CASE
MANAGEMENT

SAGE HUMAN SERVICES GUIDES, VOLUME 58

SAGE HUMAN SERVICES GUIDES

A series of books edited by ARMAND LAUFFER and CHARLES D. GARVIN. Published in cooperation with the University of Michigan School of Social Work and other organizations.

A **SAGE** HUMAN SERVICES GUIDE **58**

THE PRACTICE
OF CASE
MANAGEMENT

David P. MOXLEY

*Published in cooperation with the University of
Michigan School of Social Work*

SAGE Publications
International Educational and Professional Publisher
Newbury Park   London   New Delhi

For information address:

 SAGE Publications, Inc.
2455 Teller Road
Newbury Park, California 91320
E-mail: order@sagepub.com

SAGE Publications Ltd.
6 Bonhill Street
London EC2A 4PU
United Kingdom

SAGE Publications India Pvt. Ltd.
M-32 Market
Greater Kailash I
New Delhi 110 048 India

Printed in the United States of America

Library of Congress Cataloging-in-Publication Data

Moxley, David
    The practice of case management / David P. Moxley.
      p. cm.—(Sage human services guides series ; v. 58)
    ISBN 0-8039-3205-7
    1. Social case work—United States—Management. 2. Social work administration—United States. I. Title. II. Series: Sage human services guides ; v. 58.
    HV43.M65   1988
    361.3'2'068—dc19   89-4217
                                                  CIP

96 97 98 99 00 01 15 14 13 12 11 10

Contents

Acknowledgments

It is difficult for me to enumerate all of the people who have contributed to the preparation of this book. Many have assisted me, directly and indirectly, including both students and colleagues. Countless interactions over the past three years have shaped many of my ideas about case management. Those agencies that have invited me to consult with them regarding case management and interdisciplinary practice provided forums within which I could test a number of my ideas. These agencies are too numerous to list but I want to thank them all for the opportunities they afforded me.

Some of my core ideas regarding the practice of case management were worked out four years ago while I was on the staff of Southwest Community Health Centers, Columbus, Ohio. The case managers of this mental health agency were gracious enough to allow me to consult with them in the design of a case management system. Two people at this agency were significant resources. Judy Sillince, who directed the case management program, helped form my thinking about the integration of formal services and social support systems while Martha Knisley, who was the Associate Executive Director of Southwest, introduced me to community support concepts and principles.

Other individuals also deserve acknowledgment. Professor Paul P. Freddolino of the Michigan State University School of Social Work served as an attentive, supportive colleague during the preparation of the manuscript. Also, I want to acknowledge Dean Leon Chestang of the Wayne State University School of Social Work for his indirect support.

Finally, I want to dedicate this book to two people. First, to Jack S. Friedman, an architect who is always willing to chat about the design of social interventions. Second, to my mother, Sarah Rose Winokur Moxley.

Chapter 1

The Role of Case Management in the Human Services

KEY QUESTIONS

1. What do case managers attempt to achieve on behalf of their clients?
2. What is meant by case management as a "client level" strategy for the coordination of services?
3. What is meant by the coordination of services?
4. How is "cross-sectional" continuity of care different from "longitudinal" continuity of care?
5. What factors create a need for case management?
6. Why are case managers described as "boundary spanners"?
7. What are the three components of the client support network?
8. What are the five practice functions of case managers?

PURPOSE OF THE BOOK

This book is a guide for human services practitioners who are learning about case management as they train to fill case management roles. The book also is an appropriate in-service guide for case managers seeking to augment their skills.

The purpose of this book is to assist you in building your knowledge and skills as a case manager. My goals are to:

1. Emphasize the important role case management serves in contemporary human services.
2. Identify a general framework for the practice of case management that can serve as a foundation for developing your own approach.
3. Identify and elaborate the major functions of case managers by outlining "what case managers do" and "how they do it."

Although a social work practitioner and educator, the author recognizes and values the plurality of roles within the human services. Consequently, I have developed a guide that is appropriate for practitioners trained at either technical or professional levels.

The general framework of case management I propose also is appropriate for practitioners working in different human service settings or delivery systems. Thus, health care workers, mental health workers, rehabilitation personnel, and professionals providing case management services for the elderly should find the framework relevant to their practice.

INTRODUCTION TO CASE MANAGEMENT

Across the many fields of human services today, case management is gaining recognition as a major practice strategy essential to promoting effective service delivery to diverse target populations. To cite just a few of these areas, case management is being employed in homebased care, mental health, vocational rehabilitation, aging, and developmental disabilities (Roessler & Rubin, 1982; Sanborn, 1983; Steinberg & Carter, 1983; Zawadaski, 1984).

Although these are diverse fields of human services practice, the rationale for employing case management and its definition across these fields is remarkably similar. The rationale for case management is based on the notion that human services practitioners often work with people who have multiple needs as a result of severe disability or handicapping conditions.

Organizing services to address these needs, and subsequently fulfilling them, can require the involvement of various delivery systems such as housing, employment, mental health, social services, and health care. Assembling these services and managing their coordination are the responsibilities of case managers.

Clients of case managers often have significant disabilities limiting their capacities to locate this assistance on their own, to bring services together in compatible and coherent ways, to negotiate with many different providers, and to sustain these services or benefits over time. Case managers assist their clients in undertaking these tasks by assessing a client's needs, by identifying appropriate services, opportunities, or benefits, by developing a comprehensive plan of services, by advocating for a client's access to and use of services, and by monitoring or evaluating the appropriate and effective delivery of these services. Reflecting on the complexity of such tasks and of the systems with which case managers work, one is impressed with the sophisticated skills and knowledge required of these human service professionals (Levine & Fleming, n.d.).

Kanter (1985) discusses how this rationale for case management is operationalized within the mental health field for persons who have severe psychiatric disorders:

> (People with severe psychiatric disorders) require a wide range of treatment and rehabilitation approaches that include medication, psychotherapy, family involvement, day treatment, crisis intervention, and brief and extended hospitalizations. Simultaneously, they often need a variety of social services that include housing, financial assistance, vocational training and placement, and medical care. Although obtaining needed services is not easy for "healthy persons", these patients have particular difficulty in locating and negotiating such assistance. (p. 78)

The definition of case management follows from the rationale guiding the use of this practice technology. Briefly, case management can be defined as a client-level strategy for promoting the coordination of human services, opportunities, or benefits. The major outcomes of case management are: (1) the integration of services across a cluster of organizations (Goldstein, 1981); and (2) achieving continuity of care (Johnson & Rubin, 1983).

Let us examine the concepts that are basic to understanding case management. First, "client-level" means that the case manager is working on behalf of a specific person or group of persons. The person is seen as an unique individual with a unique spectrum of needs. In addition, the case manager works closely with the client (or significant others) in the identification of these needs. The services identified by the client and the case manager, therefore, are individualized according to the needs of the client.

Second, "coordination of services" means that the case manager is mobilizing services and agencies to address a similar package of client goals rather than having these agencies formulate different goals which may contradict or displace one another. Services are said to be "coordinated" when the principal actors within the helping network are in agreement with one another regarding the client's care, and are moving in the same direction. As a result of case management, services or agencies should work together harmoniously and not at cross-purposes (Goldstein, 1981).

Third, "integration" means that the case manager strives to realize a workable coherence among services offered under different organizational auspices (Goldstein, 1981). This is often achieved through the pooling of many services within a singular plan.

Fourth, "continuity of care" has two dimensions: cross-sectional and longitudinal. According to Test (1979), "cross-sectional" continuity of care means that at any given point in the person's treatment, the person is involved in a comprehensive system of care that is appropriately meeting the person's needs. "Longitudinal" continuity of care, according to Test (1979), means that the fulfillment of the person's needs continues over time.

Case management, therefore, is a dynamic strategy. In the short run, it focuses on identifying and fulfilling a spectrum of client needs within a complex organizational field. Over the long run, case management responds to the changing and emerging needs of clients as they grow, develop, or experience new challenges. This definition will be further elaborated later in this chapter.

THE NEED FOR CASE MANAGEMENT
WITHIN HUMAN SERVICES

The emergence of case management can be traced to six significant factors that influence the structure and process of service delivery within contemporary human services. These factors are (1) the impact of deinstitutionalization on human service delivery, (2) decentralization of community services, (3) the presence within our communities of client populations with significant problems of social functioning, (4) the recognition of the crucial role social support and social networks play in the social functioning of individuals, (5) fragmentation of human services, and (6) the growing concern with the cost effectiveness of human services.

DEINSTITUTIONALIZATION

Deinstitutionalization is a pivotal factor which has led to the need for case management. An attribute of delivering care within so-called "total institutions" was that all services were easily housed within one facility, and could be administered through a centralized administrative bureaucracy. Movement of people out of these facilities into community-based programs, or the return of these individuals to their natural families created a major service delivery problem. Whereas in the total institution the many services required by people were geographically and administratively centralized, this is not true of human services within communities.

With a few exceptions, community-based services are not under the auspices of one organization. They tend to be geographically dispersed, with each agency having its own funding and service eligibility requirements. Often there is no one comprehensive system whose purpose is to identify a client's needs and to respond comprehensively to these needs. Case management is seen as a way to offset these problems by offering a mechanism for bringing services together across organizational boundaries. In addition, there is one person (or team) who is accountable for identifying and responding to client needs. Ideally, through the provision of case management, there is a means of tracking clients as they move through a community system of human services.

DECENTRALIZATION

Deinstitutionalization has accentuated another characteristic of human services that intensifies the need for case management. Services provided within community settings are decentralized, with few mechanisms existing for the integration of these services or for the coordination of the many agencies whose services are potentially relevant to clients (Aiken, Dewar, DiTomaso, Hage, & Zeitz, 1975). From the perspectives of many clients and their families, accessing and using community services can be as difficult as untangling a Gordian knot. The case manager is often seen as the professional (or professionals) who offsets the negative effects of decentralization by organizing services across agency boundaries and by holding agencies accountable for serving a client (Quinn, Segal, Raisz, & Johnson, 1982).

SERVICE POPULATIONS WITH MULTIPLE NEEDS

Compared to several years ago, there are many more people with major disabilities or major problems in social functioning living within our communities. This is a third factor creating a need for case management. Having mental retardation, mental illness, physical disability, or serious medical problems can create many needs. It is difficult for such individuals to achieve social integration and to master the many demands of community living without receiving multiple services and supports.

Income, employment, housing, socialization, transportation, and obtaining the necessities of daily living are needs that people with serious problems in social functioning confront on a frequent basis. Typically, these needs cannot be addressed by one agency or service system (such as a state department of mental retardation). The reality is that many people with disabilities have needs which, if they are to be fulfilled, may require the involvement of several service sectors.

Case managers are frequently called upon to assist in organizing these services as a means of enabling a person to live within a community setting. Case managers can also serve preventive functions by identifying and mobilizing support services or emergency services that will divert a person from entering an institutional setting (Moxley, 1984).

FRAGMENTATION

Coordinating services across multiple sectors is not an easy task because of a fourth factor. Many of our human services are organized according to a categorical logic. State and local human service departments may be organized according to age groups (e.g., children, aged), according to functional areas (e.g., health, mental health, employment, housing), or according to problem areas (e.g., corrections, mental retardation). Consequently, one must have a specific type of problem or disability, or fall within a specified target population, to access a particular human service system.

Many of us have experienced the frustration of getting one state or local agency to serve a client whose care is perceived as the responsibility of another agency. Obtaining mental health care for a person who has mental retardation or obtaining bureau of vocational rehabilitation services for a person with a major psychiatric disability can be extremely difficult for human service professionals, let alone a client, to achieve. It is often difficult within our human services to move beyond the category to which the person has been administratively assigned to a place where providers work collaboratively across major state or local departments to identify and address the needs of a client in an integrated manner (Lipsky, 1980).

Without such integration, human services are said to be fragmented. That is, they do not easily fit together. Consequently, there is a failure to comprehensively address the needs of clients within a unified system of care (Goldstein, 1981; Gilbert & Specht, 1974). Case management is seen as a mechanism to counteract fragmentation at the level of the client. Case managers frequently work toward the goal of getting providers from categorical systems to work together on behalf of a client whose needs cut across these systems.

SOCIAL SUPPORT AND SOCIAL NETWORKS

A fifth important factor in considering the need for case management is the growing awareness among human service professionals of the effects of social support and social networks on the quality of life of our clients. Often referred to in the professional literature as the "informal system of care," many of our clients receive tangible assistance, guidance, and emotional support from family, extended kin, friends, or lay helpers (Caplan, 1974).

Such social support provided by caring individuals can have a significant impact on enhancing a person's health, mental health, and community living (Whittaker & Garbarino, 1983). Alternatively, support from significant others can have a negative or neutralizing effect on the benefits obtained from human services. Within our human service systems there are few mechanisms for integrating the provision of formal services with social support provided through the client's own social network (Curtis, 1979).

Case management can serve as a mechanism for bridging informal and formal systems of care. Case managers can play significant roles in the coordination of those individuals or social institutions providing informal support with the work of professionals who provide formal human services.

COST CONTAINMENT

The sixth factor creating a need for case management is the growing concern for containing costs of human service delivery while maximizing the impact of service delivery within the constraints of scarce resources. Decentralization of human services makes the monitoring of costs and related service duplication at the client level a difficult enterprise. A case manager who manages the overall plan of care and who has the power to authorize the purchase of services from community agencies is seen as a means of containing costs while maximizing effective service delivery (Zawadaski, 1984).

THE WORK OF CASE MANAGERS

From this review of the factors creating a need for case management it is apparent that this form of human service practice is designed to strengthen the functioning of human service delivery so that individual clients can realize a better, more continuous, system of care.

The work of case managers requires them to frequently engage in "boundary spanning." This term, borrowed from the literature on complex organizations, refers to the case manager moving across the boundaries of agencies, organizations, or systems to process or gather client information, to negotiate the transaction of resources on behalf of the client, to obtain accountability for service delivery, and to monitor or evaluate the outcome of services (Hasenfeld, 1983).

Given the limitations and problems clients can experience in attempting to obtain and combine services from multiple human service organizations, the work of case managers as boundary spanners becomes crucial. Some of the activities case managers can use in operationalizing the boundary spanning role include:

1. Coordinating client-level goals, services, and information across (1) human service organizations, (2) major sectors of human services, and/or (3) across formal and informal service sectors.

2. Serving as a "fixed point of responsibility" for clients so they have one specific professional (or team of professionals) to look to for assistance. In addition, providers and social network members can look to the case manager for information about client needs and the services being provided to fulfill these needs.

3. Serving as a self-correction mechanism for human service providers and members of the client's social network by providing evaluative feedback regarding the appropriateness or impact of services and social support activities.

4. Obtaining access to services for clients who may "fall through the cracks" of a categorical service delivery system, or for clients who may not fit into existing categories because of multiple problems.

5. Undertaking capacity-building activities designed to help clients to move toward higher levels of functioning or to increase their independence by (1) helping social network members provide support to their dependent member, and (2) by assisting human service providers in the delivery of accessible, appropriate, and adequate services (Steinberg & Carter, 1983).

6. Feeding client-level or caseload needs assessment information into the planning of human services within the community.

7. Identifying and reducing service duplication within client service plans, thereby enhancing the cost-effective delivery of human services.

Implied in this listing is that the case manager takes a "systems perspective" in relationship to clients and their environments. The activities of the case manager involve the broad picture. The case manager is concerned with the interaction of the client with both the human service sector and with social networks, and focuses on whether these structures are working toward the fulfillment of client needs.

A FRAMEWORK OF CASE MANAGEMENT PRACTICE

The information presented above can be synthesized into a framework of case management practice. This framework has three major components. The first component is a formal DEFINITION OF CASE MANAGEMENT. The FOCUS OF CASE MANAGEMENT is the second component. The third component consists of the PRACTICE FUNCTIONS OF CASE MANAGEMENT.

DEFINITION OF CASE MANAGEMENT

Case management is defined within this guide as a designated person (or team) who organizes, coordinates, and sustains a network of formal and informal supports and activities designed to optimize the functioning and well-being of people with multiple needs. Through these activities the case manager seeks to accomplish the following goals:

1. To promote when possible the skills of the client in accessing and utilizing these supports and services.
2. To develop the capacities of social networks and relevant human service providers in promoting the functioning and well-being of the client.
3. To promote service effectiveness while attempting to have services and supports delivered in the most efficient manner possible.

FOCUS OF CASE MANAGEMENT

Figure 1.1 presents a multi-functional framework of case management practice. The framework is designed as a circle to indicate that the process of case management is not necessarily linear or sequential. Functions can be undertaken in any order providing the needs of the client are first iden-

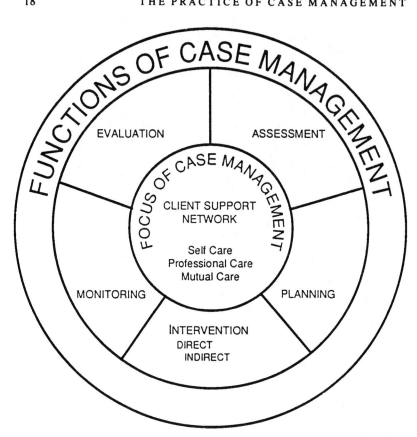

Figure 1.1. A Multi-Functional Framework of Case Management Practice.

ti.fied by the case manager. During certain periods of the case management process, however, one function may be given priority over others.

All the functions are critical to the development of the core of case management. This core is labeled as the FOCUS OF CASE MANAGE-MENT: this is what the case manager is seeking to create through the application of case management functions. The focus of case management is the creation of a CLIENT SUPPORT NETWORK involving the integration of three components:

1. The ability and capacities of the client to engage in self-care activities and tasks. This is the SELF-CARE COMPONENT of the client support network.

TABLE 1.1 Exemplary Case Management Activities

Case Management Functions	Dimensions of the Client Support Network		
	Self Care	Professional Care	Mutual Care
Assessment	Assess daily living needs, physical mobility, social and interpersonal skills, mental health status, and capacities to advocate for self.	Obtaining assessments from disciplines, assessing eligibility criteria of human services, identifying availability of human services, assessing skills of providers to work with client.	Assess structure of social network, assess sentiment toward the client within the network, identify natural helpers, identify types of social supports available.
Planning	Target improvement of client skills and capacities, plan for improvement of functional status and quality of life.	Target utilization of relevant human services and address the accessibility, availability, and appropriateness of these services.	Target involvement of social network members and the provision of social support.
Intervention	Teach client, when possible, to advocate for own needs and interests, teach client to become more involved in own care.	Broker services, coordinate services, advocate for responsiveness to client needs, build capacities of human service providers.	Consult with network members in the provision of support, arrange supportive services for network members to reduce stress, assist network members in skill development.
Monitoring	Monitor indicators pertaining to client skill and capacity building.	Monitor whether services are being provided according to the case management plan.	Monitor the provision of social support and the involvement of social network members.
Evaluation	Evaluate whether the client's functional status, quality of life and satisfaction with services are improving.	Evaluate whether services have made an impact on the functional status and quality of life of the client.	Evaluate the impact of social support on the functioning of the client.

2. The involvement of multiple professional providers in the delivery of services. This is the PROFESSIONAL CARE COMPONENT of the client support network.
3. The involvement of the client's social network in the provision of care and social support. This is the MUTUAL CARE COMPONENT of the client support network.

THE PRACTICE FUNCTIONS OF CASE MANAGEMENT

The client support network is organized, coordinated, and sustained through the application by the case manager of five key case-management functions. The case manager may undertake the functions in a different order and may repeat some if the needs of the client require such repetition. The case manager may also move sequentially and rapidly through the functions as a means of responding to a major client need or to a crisis situation. Table 1.1 presents exemplary case management activities organized by case management functions and by the dimensions of the client support network. These key functions are discussed next.

1. Assessment

Case managers are involved in comprehensive assessment activity involving the (1) assessment of client self-care capacity and human service needs; (2) assessment of a client's social network and its capacity to respond to the client's needs; and (3) assessment of human service providers and their capacity to respond to the needs of the client.

2. Planning

Case managers are involved in developing comprehenisve service plans that can integrate the services and social support activities of many providers and social network members. These plans are based on either multidisciplinary or interdisciplinary process and involve substantial input from clients and members of their social networks.

Planning client service delivery includes (1) the delineation of major needs; (2) the translation of needs into service delivery and social support goals and objectives; (3) the identification of service delivery and social support roles and responsibilities; (4) the establishment of timelines; and (5) the identification of indicators of effectiveness through which the case manager (or a case management team) can monitor and evaluate the plan of service.

TABLE 1.2   Overview of Case Management

---

1. DEFINITION OF CASE MANAGEMENT

A designated person or team who organizes, coordinates, and sustains a network of formal and informal supports and activities designed to optimize the functioning and well-being of people with multiple needs.

2. GOALS OF CASE MANAGEMENT

Promoting when possible the skills and capacities of the client in accessing and utilizing human services and social supports.

Developing the capacities of social networks and relevant human service providers in promoting the functioning and well-being of the client.

Promoting service effectiveness while attempting to achieve efficient service delivery.

3. SIGNIFICANT FACTORS INFLUENCING NEED FOR CASE MANAGEMENT

Deinstitutionalization and movement to community-based care.

Decentralization of community services.

Presence of client populations with significant problems of social functioning.

Recognition of the important role of social support and social networks in promotion of a person's well-being.

Fragmentation of state and local services.

Growing concern with the cost-effectiveness of human services.

4. FOCUS OF CASE MANAGEMENT

Formulation of client support network that integrates (1) client skill development; (2) involvement of social networks; and (3) involvement of multiple providers.

5. PRACTICE FUNCTIONS OF CASE MANAGERS

Assessment of (1) client service needs; (2) social network capacities; (3) capacities of human service providers.

Development of comprehensive service plan based on multidisciplinary or interdisciplinary professional involvement and substantial client involvement.

Intervention directly with client as a means of enhancing skills and capacities for self-care and/or indirectly with systems impinging on client.

Monitoring of service plan implementation and tracking of client status, service delivery, and involvement of social network members.

Evaluation of service plan effectiveness and its impact on client functioning, on social network's capacity to support client, and on capacity of human service professional to work with client (and similar clients).

---

3. Intervention

Case managers are involved in the delivery of interventions designed to change either the client, the client's social network, or the performance of human service providers. Two types of intervention are employed by case managers. DIRECT INTERVENTION occurs when the case manager works with clients usually in an effort to enhance their skills and capacities for accessing and using services. Examples of direct case management interventions include (1) teaching the client communication and self-expression skills; (2) teaching the client self-advocacy skills; and (3) intervening during periods of crisis.

INDIRECT INTERVENTIONS are used by the case manager in changing the behavior or performance of a system on behalf of the client. Examples of this type of intervention include (1) linking clients to human service providers; (2) brokering services; (3) advocating for responsiveness to client needs; and (4) increasing the provision of social support.

4. Monitoring

Case managers are involved in monitoring the implementation and accomplishment of the client service plan. The case manager seeks to track (1) the status of the client; (2) the planned delivery of human services; and (3) the involvement of social network members. Through monitoring activities, the case manager seeks to judge the extent to which the client service plan is being implemented in the prescribed manner.

5. Evaluation

Case managers evaluate the impact of the service delivery plan on the client. The case manager uses qualitative and quantitative techniques in judging whether, and to what extent, the client is experiencing benefits from the implementation of the service plan. The major evaluation question for the case manager is whether the plan is an effective one. That is, one that is improving the functioning or well-being of the client.

Other evaluation questions may include (1) the extent to which social network members are developing competencies in supporting the client; and (2) the extent to which human service providers are improving their competencies to serve similar clients.

Table 1.2 summarizes the overall approach to case management outlined in this chapter. The focus and functions of case management serve as the major organizing themes for the remaining chapters.

CONCLUSION AND OVERVIEW OF THE BOOK

The logic of case management presented in this book is consistent with the ecological paradigm emerging within many fields of human service

(Whittaker, Schinke, & Gilchrist, 1986). This paradigm emphasizes the need to gain a transactional understanding of individuals within the context of their environments (Bronfenbrenner, 1979; Germain & Gitterman, 1980). Building the skills of clients while simultaneously promoting the provision of social support, and increasing the accessibility and usefulness of human services are primary concerns of case managers who operationalize this paradigm within their practice.

This chapter has made clear that case management is not simply an administrative function designed to process clients more efficiently. As conceptualized within this chapter, case managers engage in proactive roles within the human services. Through such activities as trouble-shooting problems clients experience with human services, coordinating services, and evaluating services case managers can contribute to enhancing the functioning of human service delivery systems.

The remaining chapters of this text examine each major function of the case manager. Emphasis is given to the use of these functions in formulating and sustaining the client support network. Chapter 2 elaborates on the assessment of client needs and the integration of needs assessment with the assessment of social networks and human service systems.

Chapter 3 discusses the planning of comprehensive service delivery. Chapter 4 examines the direct intervention function of case managers, and Chapter 5 examines the indirect intervention function. Chapters 6 and 7 discuss the monitoring and evaluation functions, respectively. Brief practice guidelines are outlined in Chapter 8.

EXERCISES

1. Select a client from your current case load. List the current needs of this client. You may want to use the following categories in organizing these needs: (1) health, (2) mental health and psychological, (3) housing and shelter, (4) employment and income, (5) transportation, (6) nutritional, (7) socialization and interpersonal, and (8) leisure and recreational.

2. After listing these needs indicate the agencies that are most appropriate to respond to the identified needs of your client. Also, list members of the client's social network who can assist the client in meeting his or her needs.

3. List at least five ways that you engage in "boundary spanning" on behalf of your clients.

4. Describe how you implement each of the five case management functions in your current human service work.

Chapter 2

Assessment of Client Service and Support Needs

KEY QUESTIONS

---

1. What is meant by the concept of assessment?

2. Why is the assessment of client needs an important function of case management?

3. Why is needs assessment described as dynamic?

4. What are the seven key attributes of needs assessment?

5. In what ways can case managers involve clients in the assessment process?

6. What are the major needs that case managers assess?

7. How do case managers assess the self-care capacities of their clients?

8. How do case managers assess the mutual care resources available to their clients?

9. What are the major forms of social support that case managers seek to assess?

10. How does the case manager assess professional care resources?

11. What is the role of the resource matrix in the process of case management assessment?

THE IMPORTANCE OF ASSESSMENT IN CASE MANAGEMENT

As discussed in the first chapter, case managers often work with people who have multiple needs and who may not be able to meet these needs by themselves. Obtaining housing, employment, recreation, and income are examples of the needs that clients of case managers may confront. These daily living needs may be addressed by identifying sources of informal support through which needs can be fulfilled or by identifying services, benefits, or opportunities that are delivered through formal human services.

For the case manager and the client to identify requisite services they must begin by assessing the person's basic service and support needs. Assessment of client needs, therefore, is a critical function of case managers. The author emphasizes both service and support needs in order to draw a distinction between the different roles of formal human services, informal social network resources, and self-care in responding to the needs of clients. Consistent with the framework of case management presented in the first chapter, case managers address the questions of "What needs can be fulfilled through the client's own initiative and care?," "What needs can be fulfilled through the client's existing network of social support?," and "What needs can be fulfilled through existing human services?"

Assessment also is an important function for case managers because, as implied above, it is a primary means through which case management is individualized to address the unique needs or concerns of clients. Recognition of such individualization and uniqueness underscores the importance of case management taking a client-level perspective.

Finally, needs assessment is an important function because it enables the case manager and the client to develop an information base from which to plan for need fulfillment. By identifying the basic and life-enhancing necessities of the client, the case management process can translate this information into goals and objectives that will subsequently direct case management intervention. But before case managers can help to improve a person's situation, they must understand the needs of that client. This principle is consistent with the idea of case management as a "client-level" service strategy.

GOALS OF CHAPTER

With the foregoing rationale guiding our understanding of the importance of needs assessment in the case management process let us focus on the goals of this chapter, which are as follows:

1. Identify a general needs assessment strategy for case managers and identify the general attributes of this strategy.
2. Identify the needs of clients that serve as the foci of assessment.
3. Expand this strategy by discussing the assessment of self-care, mutual care, and professional care resources.

OVERVIEW OF ASSESSMENT

Assessment is the process by which the case manager and the client cooperate in the collection, analysis, prioritization, and synthesis of information concerning the identified needs of the client (Hepworth & Larsen, 1982). Assessment begins as an exploratory process and results in a formal statement of client needs. This formal statement remains dynamic and is revised over time as the client's needs are fulfilled or change in nature and extent. The goal of the case manager is to conduct an assessment that will not only identify client needs, but will also identify the attributes of the situational context for fulfilling these needs. In other words, the case management assessment process attempts to achieve the following:

1. The identification of the extent and nature of client needs.
2. The identification of the capacity of the client to address these needs.
3. The identification of the capacity of the client's social network to address these needs.
4. The identification of the capacity of human services to address these needs.

The distinction here between the concept of assessment and the concept of diagnosis is important. Too often human service professionals are preoccupied with the pathology or dysfunction of the client. Emphasis is placed on "what the client cannot do" or "the personal deficiencies of clients which cause their problems." Such preoccupation is indicative of a "diagnostic approach."

Alternatively, assessment is a more positive concept that recognizes the client's limitations while seeking to identify the strengths of the situation that can lead to client growth and development. During the process and episodes of assessment the case manager is alert for strengths, either within the client or within the environment of the client. Thus, case managers develop a strong appreciation for the situational context of their clients and how these contexts work or do not work toward need fulfillment.

During the process of assessment the case manager works with the client in identifying those needs which are most salient to the living situation of the person. Client perception is important here. Case managers obtain considerable information from clients about their living situations. Yet this does not mean that case managers will confine their collection of information to the client alone.

The case manager will incorporate a number of different data collection strategies. Some of these include direct interviews with the client, interviews with other human service professionals, review and analysis of official service records, and interaction with members of the client's social network. During the process of needs identification the case manager and the client review this information and compare it to the client's perceived needs. Information pertaining to the client's own strengths as a person in fulfilling these needs (such as motivation, emotional characteristics, interpersonal skills, and stress management skills), the strengths of the client's social network, and the capacities of existing human services and benefits will be organized according to major needs of the client. Table 2.1 summarizes data collection strategies that can be used by case managers.

The case manager will not be the only professional involved in the assessment process. The case manager will frequently arrange for other human service professionals to conduct specialized assessments such as psychological, psychiatric, medical, recreational, vocational, and environmental evaluations. These types of assessments will be discussed later in this chapter.

Throughout the needs assessment process the client is actively involved in providing, reviewing, and prioritizing information. A major role of the client lies in validating the collection and analysis of the assessment information (Hepworth & Larsen, 1982). One outcome of the assessment process is an agreement between the case manager and the client concerning salient needs, and the strengths and limitations of the client's situational context in meeting these identified needs.

KEY ATTRIBUTES OF CASE MANAGEMENT ASSESSMENT

The preceding overview suggests seven key attributes of the assessment process undertaken by case managers. This list can be used in evaluating the content of a needs assessment, and can be employed as a template for guiding the formulation of an assessment. The key checkpoints are:

TABLE 2.1   Examples of Data Collection Strategies for Use in Needs Identification

---

1. Verbal Description of Needs Provided by Client
   The client can be asked by the case manager to describe needs, to express feelings and thoughts, to identify resources, and to identify significant events relating to the current needs assessment.

2. Collateral Information about Needs Provided by Social Network Members
   A client's significant others may be interviewed by the case manager as a means of identifying needs and resources of the client.

3. Direct Observation of the Client's Environment
   The case manager may visit the client in his or her living situation and observe the client's immediate surroundings directly.

4. Contacting Previous Providers
   With the permission of the client, the case manager may contact other human service providers who have served the client in the past. These interviews can focus on the nature and outcomes of previous services.

5. Review of Agency Records
   The case manager may review client records maintained by agencies that have served the client in the past.

6. Obtaining Information from Testing
   Depending on the professional credentials of the case manager, he or she may administer health, developmental, mental health, educational, or other instruments as a means of obtaining needs assessment information. Alternatively, the case manager may arrange for other professionals to conduct such assessments as needed.

ASSESSMENT IS NEED-BASED

The fact that case managers are concerned with the individualized needs of their clients reflects the need-based nature of the case management assessment process. Yet, at this juncture it is important to define what is meant by "need." First, needs will be influenced by the uniqueness of an individual's personal history and psychological make-up. Second, needs will be influenced by the group membership and social position of the person. Case managers frequently work with people who may be disenfranchised or who may experience discrimination or neglect. By virtue of these social forces, clients of case managers can have a range of unmet needs.

A "need" is the lack of a resource that is essential to attaining an adequate lifestyle. Such an observation is consistent with Scriven's definition of a need as ". . . anything that is essential for a satisfactory mode of existence, anything without which the mode of existence or level of performance would fall below a satisfactory level" (cited in Stufflebeam &

Shinkfield, 1986, p. 318). As Gil (1976a) emphasizes, people require the fulfillment of life sustaining needs to maintain their basic biological integrity, and require the fulfillment of life-enhancing needs to achieve actualization as human beings.

Gil (1976b) provides a framework within which the needs of clients can be better understood:

> First, there are universal, biological needs and a drive for a sense of security to have these needs met. Next there are needs for reciprocal, caring social relations; not to be isolated but to belong as a whole being, to community; to be known to, and to know others, to be acknowledged for what one is and to so acknowledge others. Finally, there are needs to discover, express, and actualize oneself through meaningful, creative, and productive activity. (p. 49)

Lack of need fulfillment can evolve into personal problems for people and into social problems for society if the needs of groups of people are not fulfilled (McKillip, 1987). One problem for a case manager to address is defined as an inadequate level of a need or a need that is not being fulfilled. The implication for case management assessment is important here. By identifying or assessing needs, the case management process sets the stage for resolving a client's problems as these pertain to his or her biological, social, and psychological status. The purposeful identification of a client's needs, therefore, is a major step toward the solution of a person's problems of daily living. A subsequent section will outline a master list of relevant needs which can guide case managers in the assessment process.

ASSESSMENT IS HOLISTIC AND COMPREHENSIVE

The assessment process undertaken by a case manager is broad and encompasses several areas. It is holistic in the sense that the case manager covers areas of biological, social, and psychological functioning. It is comprehensive in the sense that the case manager reviews many different areas of need, and assesses the capacities of clients, their social networks, and human services to meet identified needs.

ASSESSMENT IS INTERDISCIPLINARY

Case managers do not confine the assessment process to their own expertise but move beyond the boundaries of their own role and discipline to include other professionals in the process of assessment and evaluation.

"Interdisciplinary" is an important attribute of a case management assessment because it identifies the importance of 1) including other professionals in the assessment process as a means of obtaining specialized information about a client's strengths and limitations, 2) integrating the perspectives of many different professionals into the formulation of a more comprehensive profile of client needs, and 3) building a team of professionals who will be knowledgeable of client needs and who may subsequently work directly with the client in order to fulfill these needs.

The concept of "team" means that the case manager does not merely work with the client in a one-to-one relationship. As early as the assessment phase of intervention, the case manager is coordinating client information gathered across different disciplines, and facilitating the communication of several different disciplines regarding the client.

The interdisciplinary nature of case management assessment raises the possibility of the case manager assuming several different "indirect service roles." For example, the case manager may serve as a *coordinator* assuring that all disciplines receive basic directives about the information they must provide regarding a client's status. In addition, the case manager may serve as the *team leader* who convenes an interdisciplinary team and then leads the team in formulating a comprehensive assessment profile. Finally, the case manager may work as a *manager* who is responsible for assuring that other professionals provide meaningful information in the appropriate format, and according to an agreed-upon schedule. These case management roles are often reflected in the actual written assessment product.

ASSESSMENT IS PARTICIPATORY

Self-determination is a critical value guiding the relationship between case managers and their clients. The case manager does not assume a unilateral role in the assessment process but shares responsibility, involvement, and decision-making with the client. Self-determination is defined as the right of people to exercise freedom of choice in making decisions (Hepworth & Larsen, 1982; National Institute of Handicapped Research, 1985).

This freedom of choice must be clearly reflected in the assessment process by clients having:

1. Opportunities to articulate their needs and to communicate their perception of their needs.
2. The opportunity to prioritize their needs.

3. Opportunities to choose professionals who will conduct specific evaluations.

4. The opportunity to be present and involved in all forums in which assessment information is discussed and at which decisions concerning the client are made.

The written product of the assessment complements and reflects client involvement in the process of case management assessment. The written product contains information about the client's perspectives and choices as well as information about what the client views as his or her important needs. In addition, the assessment product reflects the individualization of clients and their needs, and contains a balanced presentation of a client's strengths and limitations. The assessment process recognizes the individual as a special person whose cultural, racial, ethnic, and linguistic heritage creates a unique spectrum of needs. Last, the assessment product contains evidence that the client has thoroughly and critically reviewed the information.

In some cases the client may be unable to directly participate in the assessment process because of such factors as debilitating illness or cognitive impairment. The assessment process is expanded to include an advocate whose interests are independent of those of the case manager and of the case manager's agency. The advocate's role is to represent the interests of the client as if they were his or her own (Wolfensberger & Zauha, 1973).

ASSESSMENT IS A PROCESS

The needs of clients are dynamic and will change over time. New needs may emerge as the circumstances or living situation of the client changes. Assessment also changes in content, scope, and depth to reflect the dynamic nature of client needs.

The case management process may begin with a comprehensive assessment in which client needs are documented and incorporated into a written profile. The case manager, however, must plan for revisions in the client information base by 1) periodic review of the assessment document, 2) monitoring client needs over time to detect changes, and 3) incorporating new data collection or specialized evaluations into assessment as required by the changing circumstances of the client.

Since assessment is a process, the case manager fulfills a quality-assurance role in relationship to existing assessment information. The case manager assures that existing information provides a valid portrayal of client needs and that this information is useful in identifying the services or supports necessary to the fulfillment of these needs.

ASSESSMENT IS SYSTEMATIC

The assessment process is formal in the sense that the case manager attempts to use empirical data collection methods in obtaining relevant client needs data. The case manager is concerned about the reliability and validity of the data that are collected regarding client needs and functioning. Because critical decisions will be made from the assessment, the quality of these data is important. Case managers have at their disposal a range of tools through which to conduct the assessment process. Standardized instruments useful in assessing social functioning, interpersonal skills, and self-care skills are available for different populations or diagnostic groups (e.g., Halpern, Lehman, Irvin, & Heiry, 1982). Many of these instruments are "norm-referenced" so the case manager can compare a client's results to the results obtained by a large group of individuals who have been assessed by the same instrument. Alternatively, many instruments are "criterion-referenced" and provide information about how well a client achieves a specific standard of performance (Morris, Fitz-Gibbon, & Lindheim, 1987).

ASSESSMENT IS A PRODUCT

A case management assessment is a written document that represents a range of client needs at a particular point in time (Hepworth & Larsen, 1982). The document analyzes the type, nature, and extent of client needs, and the strengths and limitations of the client's situational context in addressing these needs. The assessment document also contains a synthesis statement. This statement defines the client's needs, and identifies the related factors that support or hinder the fulfillment of client needs. As a written document, the case management assessment is time-limited and static. Only by updating the information on which it is initially based, and by refining the factors supporting or limiting need fulfillment does the case management assessment document become a dynamic and valid tool for use in planning subsequent service-delivery.

MAJOR AREAS OF NEED

Let us now turn our attention to defining the major needs of the clients of case managers. The list below represents one conceptualization of needs

which I have found to be useful in my own practice. The eleven areas identified below represent a comprehensive listing derived from Gil's (1976a)
three major categories of biological, social, and self-actualization needs.

It is important to emphasize that these needs are not stated in terms of
services. Rather, they are stated in terms of life-sustaining or life-enhancing
necessities required by people to successfully live in a complex society (Gil,
1976a). Finally, I must point out that many of these needs overlap and interact with one another. This requires case managers to conduct a comprehensive review and interrelated assessment of the needs of their clients.

INCOME

People need money with which they can secure the necessities of life.
In our society, income is typically thought of as coming from work. Alternatively, money may be obtained through social welfare mechanisms such
as public assistance, social security, and unemployment compensation. In
addition, income may be derived through a person's network of primary
relationships. For example, a person may obtain gifts of cash or loans from
family members in order to purchase housing, an automobile, or to finance
education. Key assessment questions for case managers include the ability
of their clients to generate income by themselves, their clients' eligibility
for societal benefits, and sources of income that are transmitted through
social network resources. The case manager must be concerned about
whether a person's income is *adequate* to cover the basic necessities of life.

HOUSING/SHELTER

Our contemporary exposure to the social problem of homelessness illustrates the importance of paying close attention to the fulfillment of people's housing and shelter needs. The problem of adequate and appropriate
housing affects many different populations within our society including
families, the elderly, the disabled, and the poor or those of moderate in-
comes. Case managers should reflect on the multiple dimensions of housing needs including 1) the interaction of housing with income, 2) the person's capacity to maintain an independent housing situation, 3) the physical
accessibility of housing, 4) the location of housing within safe neighbor-
hoods, 5) the permanancy of a housing situation, and 6) and the acceptability
and psychological meaning of housing to a person.

Housing and shelter can be obtained through several different sources.
The individual client can establish his own household using support from
the case manager in locating a suitable living situation. Or, housing can

be obtained through publicly sponsored sources such as a local housing authority. Last, housing may be obtained through arrangements with members of the client's social network.

EMPLOYMENT/VOCATIONAL

These needs deal with the engagement of a person in productive activity that is socially sanctioned as important. Many of us equate employment with activity that results in income. However, employment and vocational activity can satisfy many other needs, such as our desire for social affiliation and the development of our self-concepts. Case managers must understand the employment history of their clients and the skills they have to engage in employment. The case manager can also focus on vocational development by identifying vocational guidance, evaluation, placement, and training opportunities that can subsequently lead to employment. The employment needs of a person can be fulfilled through individual initiative, through the person's social network, or through employment programs sponsored by public and nonprofit agencies.

HEALTH CARE

The maintenance of optimal health is a critical area of need. This area can be inclusive of physical, optical, and dental health and can also encompass adequate and timely preventive health care. Adequate nutrition, exercise, and physical mobility are other dimensions of this need area. Case managers must be knowledgeable of the health histories, cultural and personal beliefs about health, and lifestyle practices that influence the health of their clients.

MENTAL HEALTH

Being free of depression and anxiety, and enjoying a positive outlook are essential aspects of mental health. Also, positive mental health pertains to cognition, self-esteem, and self-concept and the integration of these attributes into a distinctive and unique personality. Case managers must pay close attention to the behavioral and subjective expressions of their clients' mental health, and how they cope with the challenges and problems they experience on a daily basis. In addition, as Gil (1976a) emphasizes, people require opportunities for meaningful, creative, and productive activity which in turn influences the self-esteem, self-concept, and affect of a client. Thus, opportunities for self-actualization are inextricably tied to the mental health needs of people.

During the assessment process case managers must work with their clients in identifying mental health needs by examining the relationship between the clients' perception of their mental health needs and the opportunities they have for fulfilling other life-sustaining and life-enhancing needs.

SOCIAL AND INTERPERSONAL RELATIONSHIPS

Tied closely to a person's mental health needs are those needs which are fulfilled through affiliation with other human beings. Social and interpersonal relationships can assist people in realizing basic psychological well-being. According to Weiss (1969), social relationships can serve five functions for people involving 1) intimacy, 2) social integration, 3) the opportunity for nurturance, 4) the reassurance of worth, and 5) assistance. Table 2.2 summarizes these functions and indicates the problems that can arise if these needs are left unfulfilled in an individual.

Because these needs intimately interact with the health and mental health status of an individual, and may be structured by the location of a person's housing and his or her access to transportation, assessment of social and interpersonal needs is crucial. It is important to understand the skills and capacities a client possesses for developing and sustaining social relationships. Understanding the characteristics of the client's existing social network and the "types of provisions" the person obtains from this network is also critical.

RECREATION AND LEISURE

Our conceptualization of needs is also inclusive of those activities essential to building the quality of life of people. Like other need areas, recreation and leisure interact with the fulfillment of mental health, physical health, and social and interpersonal relationship needs. Through recreation and leisure activities people gain opportunities for companionship, solitude, self-expression, and cognitive stimulation.

Case managers are interested in understanding the recreation and leisure interests and needs of their clients, and whether they have opportunities and skills to express these interests. Alternatively, case managers are interested in how the environmental milieu of the client supports the expression of these interests and the subsequent fulfillment of recreation and leisure needs. Assessment activities may focus on the availability of recreational opportunities, the appropriateness of these opportunities, the accessibility of these opportunities, and the acceptability of these activities to the client.

TABLE 2.2   Provisions of Social Relationships

Function of Social Relationship	Provision	Prototype	Effect on Individual If Provision Is Absent
Intimacy	Emotional integration	Marriage	
Social integration	Companionship	Colleagues, friends	Isolation, boredom
Opportunity for nurturance	Giving and receiving nurturance	Parent	Meaningless
Reassurance of worth	Feedback about competence	Colleagues, friends	Decrease in self-esteem
Assistance	Resources and services	Kin, neighbor	Anxiety, vulnerability

SOURCE: Adapted from R. S. WEISS (1969).

ACTIVITIES OF DAILY LIVING

This category encompasses those activities which are essential to the daily management of a person's life. Being able to prepare nutritious food, to bathe oneself, to dress oneself, and to maintain a household are major activities that influence a person's capacity to maintain an independent life style. It is crucial for a case manager to understand these needs and how the client is able to meet them especially if the case manager is working with his or her client in achieving or maintaining independent living. Developing an understanding of the extent to which a client can successfully undertake these activities, whether members of the social network can assist the individual in such activities, or whether there are support services available through local human service agencies becomes a crucial aspect of case management assessment.

TRANSPORTATION

Community mobility is another need crucial to independent living. Developing an understanding of a person's transportation needs and resources may range from an assessment of a person's knowledge of bus schedules and skills in using bus lines to the assessment of the involvement of social network members in coordinating a transportation schedule for the individual. In the absence of such informal and self-care resources, the case manager must assess the availability of specialized transportation programs and the eligibility standards of such programs.

LEGAL

Many clients of case managers have legal needs that can be fulfilled only through the linkage of the person to an attorney. Criminal charges, issues pertaining to competency, the protection of a person's constitutional rights, and issues involving the abuse or neglect of clients may need to be processed through the legal system. It is important, therefore, that case managers assess the nature of the legal needs of their clients.

EDUCATION

Reading, writing, and computational skills are basic and important educational competencies in our society. Case managers must be sensitive to the educational needs of their clients by assessing minimal competencies, by gathering an educational history, and by identifying the priority clients give to gaining or strengthening basic educational competencies.

Of course, some clients may have severe disabilities that preclude the attainment of basic educational skills. However, these individuals can also benefit from special educational opportunities that can assist them in gaining vocational, communication, social, and other basic developmental skills.

ASSESSMENT OF NEED FULFILLMENT THROUGH THE CLIENT SUPPORT NETWORK

The assessment of client needs makes use of the concept of the CLIENT SUPPORT NETWORK introduced in Chapter 1. The case manager begins with a comprehensive review of client needs and then explores the extent to which these needs can be fulfilled by the client, the client's social network, or through the delivery of human services.

The assessment process may yield a mix of needs that can be fulfilled through different components of the client support network or by combining different components of this network. Let us examine how a case manager makes use of each major component of the client support network in the assessment of client needs.

ASSESSMENT OF SELF-CARE

During the assessment process the case manager will be attuned to the importance of understanding the extent to which clients can resolve their own needs with assistance from the case manager. Preserving and increasing a client's self-care capacity are critical because one of the outcomes of the case management process is an increased capacity on part of clients to support themselves and to fulfill their own needs.

The case manager assesses capacity for self-care through careful assessment of a client's functional status. Of interest here is the development of an understanding of the client's ". . . purposive behavior in interaction with the environment" (Halpern & Fuhrer, 1984, p. 3). Basically, the case manager is interested in the role of a person's emotional, physical, behavioral, and cognitive capacities in fulfilling the needs which have been identified so that the person can live as independently as possible. The case manager recognizes that there is interaction between a person's capacities and the environment such that a person's living situation influences the use or lack of use of emotional, physical, cognitive, and behavioral capacities.

Included below is a checklist of self-care capacities that case managers can review in developing an understanding of the strengths and limitations of a client in meeting identified needs. The actual assessment will include only the most relevant of these capacities.

CHECKLIST OF SELF-CARE ASSETS AND LIMITATIONS

I. Physical Functioning and Status

1. Presence or absence of illness or disease.
2. Presence or absence of physical disabilities that place functional limitations or restrictions on use of limbs or on physical mobility.
3. Presence or absence of orthotics or prosthetic devices that enable person to adapt to functional limitations.
4. Availability of physical energy to engage in activities of daily living, recreation, and socialization.
5. Level of coordination, strength, stability, and endurance.
6. Presence or absence of medications that may influence motivation, physical energy, and cognitive functioning.
7. Presence or absence of physical characteristics that influence social interaction such as physical attractiveness, body build, appearance, or disfigurement.
8. Physical characteristics that are indicative of psychological or health status such as tremors, tics, and rigid muscle tone.
9. Understanding the person's sensory capacities including vision, hearing, taste, and touch.

II. Cognitive Functioning and Status

1. Reality orientation including orientation to person, place, and time; understanding cause and effect relationship; accurate perception of external events and internal thoughts and affect.
2. Intellectual capacity involving ability to understand abstract ideas, concrete thinking, ability to analyze, logical thought processes, educational achievements, fund of knowledge, vocabulary.
3. Judgment involving decision-making capacities, degree of reflection on decisions, learning from past mistakes, delaying gratification, degree of planning and forethought.
4. Flexibility and coherence of cognition including appropriate associations, integration of thought and affect, openness to new ideas, ability to analyze problems or situations from different perspectives, biases and stereotypic attitudes.
5. Values including commitment to social, religious, and/or ethical standards, prioritization of values, consistency of values with behavior.
6. Self-concept including basic beliefs about oneself, valuing of self, consistency of self-conception with reality, insight into one's strengths and limitations, ways of coping with failure.

III. Emotional Functioning and Status

1. Presence or absence of depression or anxiety.
2. Presence or absence of debilitating levels of affect.
3. Adaptive or maladaptive methods of coping with debilitating affect.
4. Style of controlling emotions including blandness of affect, verbalization of affect, excitability, and intellectualization of emotions.
5. Range of emotions including feelings of joy, anger, grief.
6. Appropriateness of affect including consistency of affect with the problems or challenges the person is experiencing.
7. Means of coping with frustration.

IV. Behavioral Functioning and Status

1. Social skills available to form and sustain relationships such as sensitivity to feelings of others, cooperativeness, and assertiveness.
2. Personal habits such as personal hygiene and cleanliness, grooming, degree of organization.
3. Listening and self-expression skills such as turn-taking, ability to express one's desires, willingness to express views, attending to what others have to say.
4. Accepting personal responsibility for actions, following through on responsibilities.

5. Level of motivation involving a desire to achieve and accomplish and to improve self, being able to set goals and make progress toward them.
6. Behavioral reactions to frustration, anxiety, or depression.
7. Presence or absence of aggressive behavior.

ASSESSMENT OF MUTUAL CARE

Mutual care involves the support people receive through their social networks; that is, the range of people or institutions with whom clients interact and sustain relationships. Social networks that transmit positive social support can assist people in maintaining and augmenting their physical and psychological health (Maguire, 1983).

Why can social network support have such an influential impact on a person's ability to better cope with the demands of daily living? Caplan (1974) defines a support network as "an enduring pattern of continuous or intermittent ties that play a significant part in maintaining the individual over time" (p. 7). A highly supportive social network can buffer people from stress for a number of reasons. Weiss (1969, 1974) writes that a network of relationships provides a person with a "sense of security and place" from which a person can obtain psychological reassurance during periods of demand. Within such networks individuals are likely to be treated in individualized and personalized ways thereby enhancing their worth as people (Caplan, 1974; Weiss, 1974).

A supportive network can also supply consistent communication and feedback to an individual (Caplan, 1974). Values and expectations are usually well-defined within such network and consistent communication about behavioral expectations can serve as a means of social control (Mitchell, 1973). This normative influence can enable an individual to maintain equilibrium (i. e., behavioral consistency) during periods of stress, crisis and change. That is, during periods when communication, feedback, and information can be easily disrupted for the individual. The social support network can serve a social control function since it can act as a storehouse of cultural information and cues and thereby offer guidance and direction to a person in interpreting and reacting to a problematic situation. As noted by Weiss (1974), "membership in a network of common-concern relationships permits the development of pooled information and ideas and a shared interpretation of experience" (p. 23).

On a more fundamental level, a social network can provide emotional support and assistance with specific tasks (Caplan, 1974; Mitchell & Trickett, 1980). Individuals who are embedded in such networks have access to persons with whom they can share and talk about stress-producing situations. These individuals can obtain valuable advice and specific resources to deal with their living situation. For optimal resolution of life situations people often require access to others who can support their self-esteem while assisting in formulation of a plan of action, providing supports to operationalize this plan, and helping the person to implement ameliorative actions (Weiss, 1974).

The degree of social support available to a person is influenced by several factors serving to buffer an individual from stress-producing situations. Support involves the availability of specific individuals who are willing to provide aid and assistance. It involves the transmission of consistent norms and values about the provision of help within a network. It involves the manner in which significant others assist individuals in mobilizing their psychological resources so that they are better able to cope with emotional difficulties. Support involves how members of a person's social network share and help the individual in executing role responsibilities and tasks (e.g., a friend helping an individual deal with job-related or family-related duties and obligations). Last, as Caplan (1974) emphasizes, a support system can provide an individual with instrumental and tangible resources including money, tools, skills, and cognitive guidance so that the individual can supplement his or her own ability to deal with daily living situations.

There are several reasons for case managers to be sensitive to the social networks of their clients and the social support mediated through these networks. First, there is a significant body of research demonstrating the positive impact of network-mediated social support on the health and social functioning of people (Bloom, 1981). Second, helping clients obtain emotional and material support through their networks may complement and expand the assistance delivered through formal human services. Third, by encouraging clients to make use of their social networks case managers may enable their clients to achieve higher levels of integration within their communities (Moxley, 1988b).

The case manager assesses the availability of social network members and the level of social support by developing a social network profile (Moxley, 1988a, 1988b). Three major areas are of interest to case managers who gather social network information from their clients, client advocates, or from social network members themselves. The three major areas are as follows:

1. Structure of the social network. Structural characteristics refer to the pattern of relationships that make up the network. Table 2.3 describes four structural characteristics of a social network.

TABLE 2.3   Structural Characteristics of a Social Network

---

1. Size

   Network size involves the number of people or other social units with whom the client has direct contact. Various criteria can be used to include a person in network membership. These criteria involve frequency of contact, mode of contact (e.g. face-to-face), the need for an ongoing relationship, degree of intimacy (Llamas, 1976; Tolsdorf, 1976; Wellman, 1979). Size of a network is an indicator of the potential degree to which an individual can obtain resources or support (Kapferer, 1969).

2. Range or Composition

   This characteristic involves the number of different types of people with whom the client interacts. For example, composition of a network may include primary kin, extended kin, friends, neighbors, and work associates. Composition is an index of the number of relationship sectors with which the client has established linkages. It serves as an index of differentiation: that is, the degree to which the client has a number of different types of relationships from which to obtain support.

3. Density

   Network density is defined as the degree to which network members know of or have ongoing relationships with each other independent of the client (Boissevain, 1974). The computation of density is the number of actual ties among network members divided by the total number of possible ties (Mitchell & Trickett, 1980). Typically, density is measured along a continuum and is used as an indicator of network integration: that is, as an indicator of potential communication among network members.

4. Dispersion

   A network's dispersion involves the location of network members in terms of either the dimensions of time or space. Dispersion is an index of the ease with which the client can make contact with network members.

---

2. *Interactional characteristics of the social network.* These characteristics refer to the nature of the relationships which exist between the client and his or her network members. Frequency of interaction and how the client feels toward network members are two of these characteristics. Table 2.4 describes the major interactional characteristics of a social support network.

3. *Social support characteristics of the social network.* These characteristics refer to the social support that is transmitted between network members and the client. Three types of support are important to the case management assessment of mutual care. These are *instrumental support* in which the client receives (or provides) assistance in resolving problems, *material support* in which the client receives (or provides) tangible goods,

TABLE 2.4 Interactional Characteristics of a Social Network

1. Diversity of Linkages

The linkages that bind network members to the client actually consist of various role relations. A linkage between the client and a network member may consist of several role relations. For example, one linkage may encompass such role relations as neighbor, employee, religion, and kinship. If a linkage serves one role relation it is described as unidimensional. It if serves more than one role relation it is described as multidimensional. The diversity of linkages is an index of the degree to which the client has accessibility to a network member (Boissevain, 1974), and the degree to which the client and a network member are bound to one another through overlapping role relationships.

2. Transactional Content (Social Support)

This aspect of a network involves the types of material, resources, or goods that are exchanged between a client and network members. Transactional content can include the exchange of instrumental and affective aid including tangible resources and services as well as advice and guidance. According to Boissevain (1974), the transactional content of a network is an index of the network's quality. That is, the potential of the network to support and help the client by providing him or her with specific resources.

3. Directedness

This network characteristic involves the degree to which affective and instrumental aid is given and received by the client. Tolsdorf (1976), for example, had clients rate the degree of instrumental and affective support which they gave and received within their networks. Directedness, therefore, is an index of reciprocity and also is an index of the flow of social support.

4. Duration

This is an index of network stability. It can be conceptualized as the length of time the client has maintained relationships with others in his or her network. Also, it can serve as an index of the degree to which a client perceives his or her relationships as changing (Mitchell & Trickett, 1980).

5. Intensity (Valence)

This interactional characteristic involves the strength of a network linkage. It has been measured by asking a client to rate the strength of feelings or perceived closeness toward each network member (Llamas, 1976).

6. Frequency

This interactional characteristic involves how often a client makes contact with network members either through face-to-face, mail, or telephone contact.

and *socio-emotional support* in which the client receives (or provides) expressions of positive affect and caring.

To collect information about a client's social network the case manager can engage the client in a structured interview using the Social Network

Interview Tool (Moxley, 1983). Briefly, the case manager explores the range of social network relationships by reviewing with the client ten relationship sectors. These are:

1. Membership of the household.
2. Primary kinship relationships.
3. Extended kinship relationships.
4. Relationships maintained through work.
5. Relationships within the neighborhood.
6. Informal relationships within the community such as with storekeepers.
7. Relationships formed through religious ties.
8. Relationships formed through clubs and social groups.
9. Relationships formed through human service organizations.
10. Relationships formed through school.

Table 2.5 contains a form that can be used by case managers to conduct this review.

The case manager and the client then delimit this social network so that those individuals perceived as most supportive are identified by the client. Clients nominate these individuals, and can indicate the order of importance of their nominations. Table 2.6 includes a form guiding the identification of important network members.

Finally, the case manager can use the forms contained within Tables 2.7 and 2.8 to indicate the characteristics of social interaction and social support for each person nominated as a key supporter. Visual review of the ratings the client assigns to the social interaction characteristics and to the frequency of exchange of social support can give the case manager and client an idea of the amount of perceived social support available.

The systematic assessment of the social support networks of clients can identify a number of assets available to clients. These include:

1. Strong supportive relationships that have endured over some time through which the client obtains (or can obtain) emotional, instrumental, and material supports.
2. Specialized relationships that provide the client with a specific type of social support. For example, the client may identify a confidant with whom personal information is exchanged.
3. A diverse social network made up of a number of people drawn from kinship, neighborhood, work, and religious sectors.
4. "Balanced" relationships in which clients provide as much support as they receive. Such reciprocity can be indicative of well-developed social skills on part of the client.

TABLE 2.5 Interview Form for Exploring Range of Social Relationships

Question: Ask client to name those people with whom he or she has been "in touch" sometime during the past year.

HOUSEHOLD (H) Who lives in your household?	How are they related to you?	WORK (W) Who are you in touch with at work?	Relationship
		Relationship code for work associates: Coworker, supervisor or boss, supervisee, other	
PRIMARY KIN (PK) Are you in touch with people from the family in which you grew up?	How are they related to you?	NEIGHBORS (N) Are you in touch with any people in your neighborhood?	
EXTENDED KIN (EK) Are you in touch with other kin?	How are they related to you?	INFORMAL RELATIONS IN COMMUNITY (C) Are you in touch with others in the community? (Probe: Like storekeepers, restaurant owners, vendors, bartenders, and so on)	

TABLE 2.5 (Continued)

RELIGION/CHURCH (R)
Are you in touch with church members?

_____

_____

Are you a member of a church or a congregation?
YES   NO
How often do you go to church
(frequency per week, month, year)

What do you do there?
_____ Social club   _____ Mass/services   _____ Paid work
_____ Lecture/discussions   _____ Volunteer work
_____ Visit with minister   _____ Visit with others
_____ Other activity (please indicate)

ASSOCIATIONS (ASSOC)
Are you a member of any social groups?
(Probe: Like clubs, unions, neighborhood groups?)
If yes, what are these?

_____

_____

SCHOOL (S)
Are you in touch with anyone at school or through a day activity program?

_____

_____

FORMAL SERVICES (FS)
Are you in touch with people who work at social service, health, or medical agencies?

_____

_____

OTHERS
Are you in touch with people who you have not identified?

_____

_____

TABLE 2.6   Form Guiding Identification of Important Social Network Members

Question: Think about all of the people with whom you are in contact on a frequent basis. Now list for me those people who are important in your life at this time. List the people who are important to you at this time whether you like them or not.

PERSON	SECTOR
1.	
2.	
3.	
4.	
5.	
6.	
7.	
8.	
9.	
10.	

SECTOR CODES

H	Household
PK	Primary Kin
EK	Extended Kin
W	Work
N	Neighbor
C	Informal relations/Community
R	Religion
ASSOC	Clubs/Social groups/Organizations
FS	Formal Services
S	School

The assessment of social networks also can indicate potential problems such as:

1. A high level of social isolation indicated by very few social network or social support relationships.

TABLE 2.7 Interview Matrix for the Identification of the Exchange of Social Support

													Initials of Network Members			
													Work Together Yes, No, Not Applicable		*Normative Content*	
													Share Memberships Yes, No, Not Applicable			
													Attend Church Together Yes, No, Not Applicable			
													Eat Out Together	*Social/Leisure/Recreation (A)*		
													Games and Sports			
													Outings and Trips			
													Television			
													Parties			
													Other			
													Transportation	*Instrumental Support*		*Exchange Content (A, B)*
													Information			
													Childcare			
													Meal Preparation			
													Services/Errands			
													Household Chores			
													Care When Ill			
													Repair			
													Help with Forms			
													Help with Finances			
													Other			
													Loan Money	*Material Support*		
													Clothing			
													Food			
													Shelter/Housing			
													Furniture, Tools			
													Other			
													Advice	*Socio-Emotional Support*		
													Listens to Concerns			
													Puts you in touch with other people			
													Inquires about well-being			
													Conversation			
													Other			

A. Frequency of exchange: 0 Never, 1 Sometimes, 2 Often
B. Direction of exchange: 1 from client to other, 2 other to client, 3 reciprocal—do it for each other

TABLE 2.8 Interview Matrix for Identification of Client Interaction with Network Members

Initials of Network Members	Duration of Relationships (Years or Months)	Frequency & Mode of Contact — VISUAL: 1. Daily 2. Several times a wk. 3. Once a wk.	Frequency & Mode of Contact — PHONE: 4. Several times a mo. 5. Once mo. 6. Less frequent	When did you last see person?	Dispersion: 1. Household 2. Same block 3. Lives in city 4. Not in area	Friend?: 1. Not a friend 2. Friend 3. Good friend 4. One of my best friends	Valence: 1. Very close 2. Close 3. Distant but congenial 4. Conflict	Accessible: 1. Can count on when need help 2. Will help but only sometimes 3. Cannot count on for help 4. Cannot decide	Changing: 0. Staying same 1. Changing for better 2. Changing for worse 3. Cannot decide

2. A dominance of one relationship sector such as primary kinship that may prevent a client from establishing other relationships or from emancipating from the family.

3. A lack of social support such that the client feels that he has no one to call on for help or assistance.

4. An overdependence on human service professionals which may decrease the client's integration into the community.

5. A lack of reciprocity in the exchange of social support so that a client is either "taking too much support from others" or "providing too much support to others."

ASSESSMENT OF PROFESSIONAL CARE

I use the term "professional care" to indicate the range of community services, human service agencies, and social welfare benefits that exist within a community (Gilbert & Specht, 1981). These resources are ostensibly designed to strengthen, supplement, or replace the supports transmitted through a person's social network and/or to strengthen the person's capacities for engaging in self-care. Professional care resources can include formal services and benefits like mental health care, ambulatory health care, transportation, meals and nutrition services, homemaker services, income maintenance and social security, day care services, assistance with utility bills, respite care, and legal services.

Using professional care resources is not necessarily the first line of strategy the case manager employs in responding to the needs of clients. In a sense, the case manager progresses in a hierarchal manner in which the needs of a client are assessed as to whether they can be fulfilled through the client's own self-care capacities or through the client's social network (Rosenfeld, 1983). In those need areas that cannot be fulfilled through self-care and mutual care, the case manager then attempts to match the needs of a client with formal professional care services. However, in all instances, the objective of the case manager is to sustain and strengthen the independence of the client.

In order to fully understand the services and benefits available through the agencies located within one's community, case managers, their agencies, or a planning entity within the community develops and maintains a *resource inventory*. This inventory is basically a data base maintained in a manual, on cards, or through a computer system. It is an organized profile of the range of formal services available to clients (Steinberg & Carter, 1983). The resource inventory undergoes, on a regular basis, updating, verifying, and expansion so that changes in the community service system are reflected in this data base.

Each agency profile making up the resource inventory contains basic descriptive information about the services offered by the agency. Here are some basic categories, adapted from Springer and Brubaker (1984), that may comprise a resource inventory profile of an agency:

1. The name, address, and telephone numbers of an agency including the addresses and telephone numbers of all branches.
2. Identification of key contact people within the agency including the executive director, key administrative personnel, and the names of intake workers.
3. Identification of the office hours of the agency and its branches.
4. Eligibility requirements of the agency and how these vary by client needs or problem, type of impairment, level of impairment, age, and income.
5. Identification of the range of services offered by the agency and a description of each service.
6. Description of the application process and the supporting materials needed to make application.
7. Identification of the cost of service and the availability of financial assistance.

A valid and reliable resource inventory can assist case managers in matching the needs of clients to requisite community services. However, the resource inventory is not the only means by which the case manager assesses professional care resources.

By making referrals to agencies and services within the community and by interacting with the administrative and direct service staff of these agencies, the case manager builds a body of knowledge that can subsequently serve a crucial role in the case management assessment process. The case manager learns about those agencies that are willing (or not willing) to respond to the needs of "difficult people." In addition, the case manager learns to identify the agencies that are willing to provide outreach, perhaps to the person's home, or to mandate that the person come to the agency for services.

These nuances in the responsiveness of community agencies to a specific client or to groups of clients may not be captured in a resource inventory. Thus, the case manager engages in a qualitative assessment of the services needed by a particular client. In developing this qualitative data base the case manager employs what I call the FIVE A's OF ASSESSING PROFESSIONAL CARE (Sorenson, Hammer, & Windle, 1979). The case manager uses each of the five A's to compare the needs of a client to the responsiveness of professional care resources within a given community. Let us briefly review each one of the five A's.

1. Availability.   This dimension of the assessment of professional care focuses on whether the type of service needed by a client exists within a specific agency. Availability can interact with the needs of a target population or with a client who requires special consideration. For example, a case manager may be working with a person who presents severe behavior problems and requires behavioral therapy to decrease these problems especially within the person's residential program. Assessment of service availability may reveal that traditional psychotherapy exists within several agencies but that behavioral therapy focusing on the amelioration of behavior problems does not exist within these agencies. Thus, a "service gap" exists for a specific client and potentially for a whole population of clients.

2. Adequacy.   This dimension refers to whether a service exists in sufficient amount to meet the needs of an identified client. A client may require homemaker services Monday through Friday from early morning through early evening so that family members can attend to their work and other responsibilities. An agency that can provide such service coverage would be described as adequate. That is, the agency can provide the homemaker service in sufficient amount to meet the needs of the identified client and the needs of the client's social network.

3. Appropriateness.   Does an existing service address the specific needs of a client in a manner which is suitable for this person? Appropriateness, therefore, focuses on suitability and on whether there is a "good fit" between the person's needs and the services available in the community to respond to the client's needs. Appropriateness addresses how sensitive the service is to the needs of a client. Lack of appropriateness can create major problems in responding to the needs of a specific client:

> Martha was a 15-year-old girl who was assessed as having severe mental retardation and severe behavioral problems compounded by blindness. The child's mother could not maintain her at home and petitioned the state to admit her to a locked ward at the public developmental center. This program was designed to provide intensive habilitation to persons with mental retardation and severe behavior problems. However, except for Martha, all of the program's clients were adults. Since the program was adult-oriented it could address only Martha's behavior problems. It could not address the developmental, educational, and emotional needs of this child.

4. Acceptability. This dimension of professional care assessment focuses on the question of whether the service meets the preferences of the client. In other words, does the client have a predilection to make use of the service (National Institute of Mental Health, 1977)? The case manager needs to understand the preferences of the client and whether the service can respond to these preferences. Understanding the role of acceptability of professional care demands that case managers understand the unique needs and concerns of their clients:

> Mr. Samuelson, a 60-year-old man with moderate mental retardation, required a community residential placement after leaving a state institution. The case managers responsible for Mr. Samuelson's housing needs arranged for a trial placement at a home whose residents were mainly young adults. After the trial placement, Mr. Samuelson reported that he wanted to refuse it. He maintained that the interests of the young residents were not similar to his own and that they were much too active for his tastes.

5. Accessibility. This dimension of professional assessment is defined as the ease with which the services of an agency can be obtained by a client (Sorenson, Hammer, & Windle, 1979). Thus, there is a general absence of barriers that would prevent the client from using the service (Gates, 1980). Several factors make up an assessment of whether a service is accessible to a client including whether the service is 1) *geographically accessible* to the person, 2) *financially accessible* to the person, 3) *socioculturally accessible* to the person, 4) *psychologically accessible* to the person, 5) *temporally accessible* to the person, and 6) *physically accessible* to the person.

These factors can be translated into the following assessment questions: Can the person obtain the necessary transportation to reach the service? Can the person afford to use the service? Does the service have the linguistic capacity to work with the person as well as the capacities to address the person's racial, ethnic, or other socio-cultural characteristics? Does the person feel welcomed by the agency and does the agency reduce the person's anxiety about using the service? Are the agency's hours of operation flexible enough to take into consideration the other responsibilities or duties of the person? And does the physical layout of the agency allow for easy use by people who have limitations on their mobility or who make use of special mobility devices?

THE RESOURCE MATRIX:
ACHIEVING A SYNTHESIS OF ASSESSMENT INFORMATION

The case management assessment process involves four major areas. The case manager works with the client in need identification, and then assesses the client's own self-care capacities and the capacities of the client's social network to meet these needs. Finally, the case manager matches client needs to existing formal human services if self-care capacities and social network resources are not available or inadequate to address the client's needs. Such an assessment process yields considerable data and information about the client and his or her situational context. How does the case manager synthesize and summarize this information?

Table 2.9 presents the *Resource Matrix*, a form that can be used by the case manager as a tool in summarizing and synthesizing the needs and capacities of the client situation. The matrix consists of the five major columns of 1) Need Area, 2) Need Statement, 3) Strengths and Limitations of the Client's Self-Care Resources, 4) Strengths and Limitations of the Client's Mutual Care Resources, and 5) Strengths and Limitations of Professional Care Resources.

"Need Area" addresses one of the eleven major need areas identified earlier in this chapter. The case manager then sythesizes a "Need Statement," which identifies the specific aspect of need that the client is experiencing within the major area. For each need the case manager then identifies the strengths of self-care, mutual care, and professional care in responding to this need. Emphasis should be placed on the identification of strengths because during the assessment process the case manager and client will identify a range of resources that can be mobilized to respond to the client's needs. Limitations are identified to indicate areas of self-care, mutual care, or professional care that are failing to contribute to the fulfillment of client needs.

Completion of the Resource Matrix provides the case manager with a holistic overview of the client's situational context. It provides a data base from which the case manager, the client, and other professionals can plan subsequent intervention.

CONCLUSION

The case management assessment process is a complex one because the case manager must cover three components of the CLIENT SUPPORT

TABLE 2.9   Resource Matrix Form

| Need Area | Need Statement | Self-Care Capacities | | Mutual Care Capacities | | Professional Care Capacities | | Other Comments |
		Strengths	Limitations	Strengths	Limitations	Strengths	Limitations	
Income								
Housing								
Employment								
Health								
Mental Health								
Social								
Recreation								
Activities of daily living								
Transportation								
Legal								
Education								
Other								

NETWORK, and must match the strengths and limitations of each component to the needs of the client. As emphasized earlier in this chapter, case managers are not necessarily diagnosticians. They do not seek to make a formal diagnosis of the client or of the client's functioning. Alternatively, case managers engage in a broad needs-based assessment by:

1. Identifying the basic living and life enhancing needs of clients.
2. Systematically gathering information about how these needs can be met.
3. Organizing assessment data and information into a resource matrix that can be used in the subsequent planning of case management interventions.

Table 2.10 presents a framework that identifies the structure of case management assessment.

EXERCISES

In order to complete the exercises listed below, select one client from your case load.

1. List the ways that you can involve the client you selected in the process of case management assessment.
2. Using the list of major needs included in this chapter identify the needs of your client.
3. List the strengths and limitations of the self-care capacities of your client. Be sure to identify strengths and limitations according to the categories of physical functioning, cognitive functioning, emotional functioning, and behavioral functioning.
4. Describe the mutual care resources of the client and the relationships of these resources to the fulfillment of the identified needs of your client. What are the strengths and limitations of social network structure? Of social network interaction? And of social support mediated by your client's social network?
5. Identify relevant professional care resources that can be used to meet client needs. Critically assess these resources according to the dimensions of availability, adequacy, appropriateness, acceptability, and accessibility.
6. Summarize and synthesize the needs and capacities of your client by completing a resource matrix. Study the completed matrix and then write a statement that synthesizes client needs and the resources the client has available to meet these needs.

TABLE 2.10 The Structure of Case Management Assessment

Characteristic of Assessment	*Identification of Client Needs*	Dimensions of Assessment		
		Assessment of Self-Care	*Assessment of Mutual Care*	*Assessment of Professional Care*
Organizing Concepts	Unmet Needs	Client Functioning	Social Networks/ Social Support	Formal Human Services
Basic Units of Assessment	1. Income 2. Housing/shelter 3. Employment/vocational 4. Health 5. Mental health 6. Social/interpersonal 7. Recreation/leisure 8. Activities of daily living 9. Transportation 10. Legal 11. Education	1. Physical Functioning 2. Cognitive Functioning 3. Emotional Functioning 4. Behavioral Functioning	1. Social network structure 2. Social network interaction 3. Emotional support 4. Instrumental support 5. Material support	1. Resource Inventory 2. Availability 3. Adequacy 4. Appropriateness 5. Acceptability 6. Accessibility
Process of Assessment	Review with client and professionals the needs of the client in key areas of daily living.	Match needs with client functional areas to assess whether client can fulfill own needs.	Match needs with mutual care resources to assess whether social network can fulfill client's needs.	Match needs with professional care resources to assess whether formal services can fulfill client's needs.

Chapter 3

Development of the Client Service and Support Plan

KEY QUESTIONS

1. What is the client service and support plan?

2. What is meant by the client service and support plan involving both process and product?

3. What are the five characteristics that highlight the importance of client service and support planning?

4. Why is the planning process a participatory one? Who is involved in the process?

5. How does the client service and support plan serve as a guidance system?

6. What is meant by evaluability, and how is this concept relevant to the client service and support plan?

7. What are the six major components of a client service and support plan? What is the importance of each component?

8. What is the role of interdisciplinary team process in the development of a client service and support plan?

INTRODUCTION

The development of a service and support plan is a critical function of case management because it is the means by which case managers work with a client in identifying the intervention activities necessary to respond to client needs. In the context of case management, planning is a systematic process of identifying meaningful goals, and of developing activities and services to respond to these identified goals. The goals delineated during the planning process are linked to client needs. Thus, case management planning is inextricably tied to those client needs identified during the assessment process.

The planning undertaken by a case manager in conjunction with a client, his or her significant others, and other professionals can be characterized as both *process* and *product*. Planning is a process because it involves a set of purposeful activities undertaken to develop a plan of services and supports. These processes may include activities such as formulating an interdisciplinary team to develop a comprehensive plan, coordinating input from multiple disciplines, involving the client in the planning process, and involving key social network members in the development of the client service and support plan (Lawrence, 1975).

Implementation of these processes results in the actual plan that will guide the provision of services and supports (Gardner, 1980). This written document not only identifies the essential goals of the delivery of services and supports, but also includes statements of specific objectives, identification of activities to achieve these objectives, identification of the actors responsible for achieving the objectives, specification of timelines, and statements of expected changes if objectives are achieved (Coulton, 1979).

GOALS OF THE CHAPTER

This overview of client service and support planning suggests the goals of this chapter. These are to:

1. Identify the importance of client service and support planning in case management.
2. Specify the major structural components of a client service and support plan.
3. Discuss the process of developing a client service and support plan.

IMPORTANCE OF CLIENT SERVICE AND SUPPORT PLANNING

The importance of client service and support planning in case management practice is highlighted by five characteristics. First, the client service and support plan lays out a *workplan and division of labor*. Requisite activities are defined by the plan, and individuals are assigned tasks and responsibilities which must be accomplished to fulfill goals and objectives. In addition, the service and support plan reinforces a division of labor among the actors making up the CLIENT SUPPORT NETWORK. The plan identifies the different roles and activities of the client, social network members, and professionals in the implementation of service and support objectives.

A second important characteristic of the service and support plan is its *participatory nature*. By virtue of involving the client, social network members, and professionals, the case manager can build commitment to the service and support plan and ultimately to the achievement of client needs by the actors identified within the plan. A key principle here is that commitment to the plan and to fulfilling client needs evolves out of participation in the development of the client service and support plan. Without input, why should these individuals make a commitment to the plan?

Accountability is a third important characteristic. Because the plan identifies the roles, activities, and timelines of actors, the case manager can assure the follow-through of key individuals. So, a fourth characteristic of the service and support plan is that it serves as a *guidance system* for the case manager. The completed plan can be used by the case manager to monitor the completion of tasks, activities, responsibilities, and the achievement of objectives. The plan, therefore, becomes a tool for monitoring the implementation of goals and objectives.

The fifth characteristic of the service and support plan is its *evaluability* (Rutman, 1984). This concept means that the goals, objectives, and activities of the plan are clear enough that the plan can be evaluated by the case manager in terms of its impact on the client. Our ultimate criterion for evaluating the relevance of a service and support plan is the extent to which it makes an impact on the fulfillment of a client's needs.

STRUCTURE OF THE SERVICE AND SUPPORT PLAN

Table 3.1 presents an example of a client service and support plan. The case manager uses this form to organize the overall approach to fulfilling

TABLE 3.1   Client Service and Support Plan

Client: _____

Need Area: _____

Impact Goal: _____

Date of Plan: _____/_____/_____

Service and Support Objectives	Actors and Implementation Activities			Timeline	Expected Changes
	Client	Social Network	Professionals		

61

client needs. This plan brings together six major components that are necessary in order to address client needs adequately and effectively and, in the process of implementation, to develop a CLIENT SUPPORT NET-WORK. The major components of the plan include (1) specification of the relevant need area to be addressed within the plan, (2) identification of the impact goal, (3) identification and listing of the service and support objectives, (4) identification of the actors who will undertake specific activities designed to achieve the objectives of the plan, (5) specification of the timeline for completion of each objective, and (6) statements of changes expected to result from the completion of each of the objectives. Each of these components is elaborated below.

NEED AREA

The case management plan is designed to fulfill the identified needs of the client. Thus, the plan should start by clearly delineating the need area that will be addressed in the plan. The assessment framework presented in Chapter 2 calls for the assessment of 11 client need areas. Addressing all of these needs within a single plan may exceed the scope and resources of the case management process. It is critical, therefore, that the needs identified within the service and support plan have been prioritized by the client and the case manager.

This prioritization process can serve as the transition from need identification to the planning of the services and supports that will be mobilized to address these needs. Because case management is conceptualized as a client-level service strategy, the priorities of clients should prevail in relationship to the fulfillment of their human needs.

If the structure of the service and support plan is based on the identified and prioritized needs of the client, the plan will be both relevant and accountable. These attributes will evolve out of the capacity of both the client and the case manager to determine whether the plan actually addresses the fulfillment of the needs that have been identified as important and pressing.

IMPACT GOALS

This component of the plan requires the case manager to specify how the delivery of services and supports will make a difference in the life of the client (Morris & Fitz-Gibbon, 1978a). In other words, it is important to specify how the client's life will be changed once his/her needs are fulfilled. The term "impact" underscores the necessity of viewing the service and support plan as being linked to client change. How will the client's living situation be improved? How will the services and supports specified in the plan make a difference in the life of the client? The effectiveness of the plan, therefore, depends on the clarity with which the impact of the plan is specified.

What are goals? From this author's perspective, goals are prescriptive statements. That is, a goal indicates what will be improved by virtue of the service and supports that are delivered. Since goals are statements of direction they will indicate to the case manager and client the specific aspect of the need that will be fulfilled. Alternatively, if the case manager and client are dealing with barriers or problems preventing need fulfillment then goals will focus on what will be decreased. Ultimately, goals are statements of the effects of the case management process on the client.

Impact goals evolve out of the "Need Statements" developed during the assessment process, and incorporated into the Resource Matrix (see Table 2.9). Remember that the need statement identifies the specific aspect of need that is not being fulfilled or that must be strengthened. Impact goals can be designed to address these need statements.

Let us examine a case example as a means of illustrating the writing of impact goals. Mrs. Williams is a 75-year-old widow who has lived in her current home for 30 years. Given the decline of Mrs. Williams's cognitive and physical functioning, the structure of the home environment threatens her safety. In addition, the house lacks accessibility, with doorknobs and steep steps that she cannot easily negotiate. Finally, the structure of the house is deteriorating somewhat, with the windows leaking and the plumbing failing. The case management assessment process reveals that Mrs. Williams can continue to live in the home if her housing needs are addressed. The case manager has an opportunity to work with Mrs. Williams to preserve her independence and self-sufficiency.

The following are some examples of impact goals that are relevant to Mrs. Williams's housing situation:

Need Area: Housing

1. To increase the safety of Mrs. Williams's house so she can continue to live independently.
2. To decrease the deterioration of the physical structure of Mrs. Williams's house so she can continue to live independently.
3. To increase the physical accessibility of Mrs. Williams's house so that she can continue to live independently.

In order to preserve Mrs. Williams's independence and self-direction as much as possible, the case manager, the client, and members of her social network also identify several impact goals that address the social and interpersonal need area:

Need Area: Social and Interpersonal

1. To increase the frequency of social contact between Mrs. Williams and her neighbors.
2. To increase the frequency of social contact between Mrs. Williams and her grandchildren.
3. To increase the frequency of social contact between Mrs. Williams and peers of her own age.

SERVICE AND SUPPORT OBJECTIVES

This component of the plan requires the case manager to specify the services and supports required by the client in order to achieve client impact goals. Service and support objectives, therefore, are linked to impact goals which, in turn, are linked to the prioritized needs of the client.

A key step in the planning process is the identification of the services and supports that are essential to making an impact on the life of the client. The case manager eventually will organize and coordinate these services and supports, and will monitor whether they are being appropriately delivered to the client. In addition, the case manager will evaluate whether the provision of the services and supports specified within the plan are leading to the achievement of the client impact goals.

Service and support objectives are written to communicate what will be delivered or provided to address the achievement of the impact goal. Typically, these objectives will identify the formal services or activities to be provided by human service agencies, or will identify the informal social supports to be provided by members of the client's social network.

Continuing with our case example involving Mrs. Williams, let us examine illustrative service and support objectives related to the impact goal of "increasing the safety of Mrs. Williams's house so that she can continue to live independently:"

1. Provide technical assistance by an occupational therapist who will assess those areas of her home that pose a risk to Mrs. Williams and recommend modifications of the physical environment.

2. Based on the recommendations of the occupational therapist make modifications to the home environment so that safety hazards are reduced.
3. Educate and train Mrs. Williams about modifying her daily household routine so that her safety is increased.
4. Involve Mrs. Williams's next door neighbor in unobtrusively monitoring her safety within the home.

The primary question relating to these service and support objectives is whether they are plausibly related to the achievement of the impact goal of the plan. In other words, by implementing and achieving key service and support objectives can the case manager be confident that the desired change will occur for the client, and that ultimately the client's particular need will be fulfilled?

Inspection of these illustrative service and support objectives reveals that they are consistent with the case manager's mission of developing a CLIENT SUPPORT NETWORK. The objectives reveal that the case manager is able to include another professional (an occupational therapist), the client (Mrs. Williams), and a social network member (Mrs. Williams's next door neighbor) in activities that will lead to the fulfillment of the client's housing need.

ACTORS AND IMPLEMENTATION ACTIVITIES

For each service and support objective listed within the client's plan, the case manager identifies key actors or agencies, and specifies the activities that these actors must undertake in order to achieve a particular service and support objective. The form presented in Table 3.1 includes space to indicate the activities of the client, social network members, and professionals (and their agencies). The structure of the form reinforces the mission of the case manager in developing a CLIENT SUPPORT NETWORK. The form, therefore, is consistent with the framework of case management presented in Chapter 1.

In this section of the plan, the case manager focuses on the question of "WHO will do WHAT" in order to achieve a particular objective. For example, one objective calls for an occupational therapist to provide technical assistance in evaluating the risk to Mrs. Williams within her home. By identifying the occupational therapist and specifying his other activities, the case manager has operationalized this objective. Operationalization of this objective may result in the following activities:

1. Joe Stevens, staff occupational therapist of Southeast Visting Nurses Association, will conduct an on-site risk assessment of Mrs. Williams's household.
2. Mr. Stevens will conduct an assessment of Mrs. Williams's capacities to make use of the household environment in a safe manner.
3. Mr. Stevens will write a report of his recommendations to modify Mrs. Williams's household environment so that it becomes compatible with Mrs. Williams's physical capacities.

Another objective calls for the education and training of Mrs. Williams in a new daily household routine that will assure her safety within her home. Actors in this situation may be both the occupational therapist and Mrs. Williams. The occupational therapist will undertake activities to task analyze the new routine and to instruct Mrs. Williams in the steps involved in this new routine. Mrs. Williams will practice this new routine and demonstrate that she is proficient in it.

This section lays the foundation of the case manager's capacity to monitor the plan and thereby assure accountability. By indicating the actors and their implementation activities, the case manager can review the plan over time and assure that individuals identified within the plan are implementing the activities necessary to the successful achievement of service and support objectives.

This section of the plan also requires the case manager to reflect on how the client, social network members, and professionals can be involved in the achievement of the service and support objectives. Perhaps in some situations only the client, a social network member, or a professional will be involved in addressing a particular service and support objective. However, in other situations all three of these actors may be involved in achieving one objective. In structuring the service and support plan, the case manager maintains a focus on developing a CLIENT SUPPORT NETWORK. Opportunities to involve clients, social network members, and professionals in a coordinated effort to achieving service and support objectives signifies a holistic approach to case management practice.

TIMELINE

Linked to each objective is a date which indicates when the objective and all accompanying activities will be achieved. This component of the client service and support plan may appear simple. Yet working out sound and reasonable timelines is crucial to addressing the needs of a client effectively. First, the timeline can indicate the urgency of a particular objective. Case managers may work with people in crisis for whom several objectives must be implemented quickly. Second, the timeline can indicate the hierarchical nature of service and support objectives and their related activities. Some objectives must be completed in order to achieve other objectives. In the example of Mrs. Williams' housing situation, the occupational therapist must evaluate the safety of the household before a training protocol can be developed to help Mrs. Williams learn a new household routine.

Finally, timelines provide another basis for monitoring the implementation of the plan (Cohen, Vitalo, Anthony, & Pierce, 1980). The case manager, for example, can use the plan as a checklist. By moving down the timeline column the case manager can check those objectives and activities that have been achieved on schedule and those that have not been achieved. He or she can then follow up with those individuals who are responsible for certain activities to inquire into the barriers or problems preventing the achievement of objectives and activities.

EXPECTED CHANGES

The logic of the case management plan requires linkage among needs, goals, objectives, and activities. The achievement of service and support objectives, and their related activities must make a difference in the life of the client. Case managers, therefore, should be cognizant of the projected changes anticipated when a particular objective and its activities are accomplished.

The final section of the Client Service and Support Plan is devoted to the projected changes. The important question here is what will change if the objective is achieved. In other words, will achievement of the objective improve the life of the client? We can project the following changes from fulfilling the service and support objectives linked to Mrs. Williams's need for increased safety within her household:

1. Through technical assistance by an occupational therapist we will gain increased knowledge of the environmental threats to Mrs. Williams's safety.
2. This increased knowledge will allow us to assist Mrs. Williams in avoiding risky situations within the household.
3. This increased knowledge also will enable us to work with Mrs. Williams's neighbor to compensate for her diminished ability to monitor herself fully within the household.

The expected changes we will realize from achieving this objective include (1) increased knowledge of environmental risks, (2) skill development on part of the client, and (3) enhanced instrumental social support. These three changes move the client closer to achieving the particular impact goal, and thereby fulfill the identified need. In the case of Mrs. Williams, she can continue to live safely in her existing household. Therefore, the ultimate goal of case management has been achieved: the promotion of the independent living and self-direction of the client.

The identification of expected changes from the achievement of particular service and support objectives leads to a stronger foundation of monitoring and evaluation. The case manager can review completed objectives to assure that they resulted in the changes as originally projected. If the expected changes were not obtained then the case manager can revise the plan so that the changes are realized. Alternatively, the case manager may evaluate critically whether the implementation activities failed to result in the projected changes. This will lead to the modification of activities.

Of importance here is that the component of expected changes assists the case manager in his or her efforts to evaluate the worth and effectiveness of the plan. This activity is crucial to the case manager's assuring that service and support objectives are relevant to client needs.

PROCESS OF DEVELOPING A CLIENT SERVICE AND SUPPORT PLAN

The client service and support plan is developed through a process involving teamwork that incorporates the client, social network members, and various professionals. This section presents several areas that are relevant to the process of developing a service plan. Included are interdisciplinary process, client and social network involvement, and the inclusion of a client advocate.

USING INTERDISCIPLINARY TEAM PROCESS IN PLANNING

Case managers do not typically work in isolation from other professionals. They often find themselves working within team contexts in order to maximize the input and expertise of other professionals and of the client. Ideally, the development of a service and support plan through team process allows the case manager to coordinate large amounts of information and input, and to integrate this input into a unified plan of service delivery (Herzog, 1985).

"Interdisciplinary" is a key concept for a case manager. Building an interdisciplinary team requires the case manager to bring together a number of different professionals, the client, and client representatives into an effort that seeks to combine the perspectives of all members into one service and support plan (Brill, 1976; Ducanis & Golin, 1979; Gardner, 1980). The concept of interdisciplinary practice is distinct from both unidisciplinary and multidisciplinary practice. Unidisciplinary practice involves only one discipline taking a very specialized and narrow view of the client whereas multidisciplinary practice involves several professionals who work independently, develop their separate plans, and then meet to share their views of the client.

Interdisciplinary teamwork requires the case manager to build an integrative process in which the people involved review client needs, and then openly share and discuss information from which a service and support plan is derived. Several assumptions guide effective interdisciplinary practice. First, the process incorporates the needs of the client as the focus of team activity. Second, the process recognizes that the needs of the client cut across the boundaries of professional disciplines and, therefore, that no one professional is dominant within the process (Gardner, 1980). Third, the process requires that each team member understand the roles and functions of the other members.

Realizing this third requirement is critical for the case manager to build an effective team because it is the specification of the roles of the team members that will influence the sharing of information, the interaction of participants, and the sharing of power within the team. Interdisiciplinary team process can potentially create a great deal of conflict because it requires professionals to cooperate, collaborate, and share authority. This is not necessarily easy for individuals who may be trained to be autonomous and individualistic in their work with clients (Mizrahi & Abramson, 1985). In addition, the "territory" of different professions may overlap and create competition for authority among certain team members (Donovan, 1984).

In using teamwork to develop a client service and support plan, the case manager strives to combine the different perspectives of team members while at the same time managing any conflict that may arise. The indicators of an effective team process are similar to those of any other effective task group. They include (1) active listening on part of members, (2) focusing on the task, (3) tolerating differences and being willing to discuss these differences, (4) using clear and simple language rather than professional jargon, (5) commitment to the human and legal rights of the members, (6) leadership designed to facilitate interaction and reduce conflict, and (7) getting to know each other on a personal basis (Gardner, 1980; Seaman, 1981).

These indicators, for the most part, can be categorized into four characteristics of effective teamwork. According to Blake, Mouton, & Allen (1987), these are:

1. Objectives. Members have a clear purpose and direction for convening as a team.
2. Coordination. Members have the skills to mesh their efforts to accomplish their purpose and objectives.
3. Communication. Facts, feelings, and perspectives of members are shared in a clear and candid manner.
4. Critique. Team members engage in an ongoing monitoring of their performance. The team accepts the expression of doubt, reservations, and criticism from members.

DEVELOPING AN EFFECTIVE INTERDISCIPLINARY TEAM

Since the interdisiciplinary team serves as the vehicle by which the case manager seeks to coordinate and integrate the input of many different people, effective teamwork is critical to the overall case management process. The process of building an effective team involves four major tasks. Each task is discussed below:

1. Bringing together a team. When planning to convene an interdisciplinary team, the case manager must be concerned with the type and number of professionals to involve in the process. The case manager has already conducted his or her own assessment and can use his or her understanding of the client's needs to identify those professionals, agency representatives, and social network members who will be important in planning client service and support goals and related objectives. One critical consideration here is the size of the group. Too large a group may overwhelm the client, reduce the willingness of the client to participate, and create problems for the processing of interdisciplinary input. The case manager can follow a basic principle of structuring effective task groups:

> A group should have the smallest number of members possible who have all the resources and points of view needed to meet the goal or mission of the group. (Stech & Ratliffe, 1985, p. 118)

The mission of the interdisciplinary team is to construct a plan of services and supports that addresses the needs of the client. Thus, the team needs to be large enough to include the disciplines or agencies that will respond to these needs, and to include the client and social network members.

The case manager, however, must be cognizant of the fact that as size increases the complexity of the team will increase, potentially making team process unwieldy.

2. Building team cohesion.   The task of developing an effective interdisciplinary team requires team members to recognize that they share an interest in responding to the needs of the client (Gardner, 1980). Cohesion will evolve out of a feeling that each participant is a valued member of the team, and that his or her input is important to formulating a relevant plan. Auvine and his colleagues (1978) identify several core attitudes that contribute to group cohesion:

1. A team contract that establishes an expectation of cooperation over competition
2. Common ownership of ideas
3. Valuing members' feelings and perspectives
4. Encouraging the contributions of all members
5. Undertaking efforts to equalize the power of all team participants
6. Recognizing that disagreement is a natural part of teamwork and can be resolved

The case manager contributes to building the cohesion of the interdisciplinary team by encouraging interaction among all participants. First, the case manager needs to make sure that the goals and agenda of the interdisciplinary team are clear, and that participants understand what is expected of them and the nature of their roles within the process (Tropman, 1980). These can be achieved through telephone contact and correspondence before the first meeting, and by providing thorough orientation and training of members early in the team process (Fox, 1987). Second, the case manager can encourage informal social interaction at the beginning of team sessions. Encouraging team members to get to know one another on a personal basis will reduce the formality of team meetings.

3. Conducting team meetings.   Once the team process is implemented, the case manager will be concerned about maximizing the productivity of the team. The major product of the process is the development of a written client service and support plan with the goals, objectives, activities, and roles of participants clearly defined.

The case manager can conceptualize each meeting as involving five major steps (Avery, Auvine, Streibel, & Weiss, 1981):

Social interaction.   This involves allowing time for human interaction and personal contact before the formal work of the team begins.

Orientation.   The team then proceeds into a brief review of what was accomplished during the previous session and what needs to be accomplished during the current session.

Structuring.   The team reviews its operational rules. Choosing the person to record team process and decision-making, identifying facilitators, and discussing the rules of introducing new assessment material or other information are important activities.

Constructive Work.   The actual work of planning then proceeds. The discussion and identification of client needs, goals, service and support objectives, activities, timelines, and expected changes will be covered during this step.

Completion.   Team members will review the progress made on the client service and support plan, review decisions, and identify tasks for the next meeting providing one is required.

4. Evaluating the effectiveness of interdisciplinary teamwork.   The task of developing interdisciplinary team process requires the participants to consciously evaluate the effectiveness of the team. Two dimensions of evaluation are important here. First, the team will examine the effectiveness of its process of interaction. Second, the team will examine its execution of the tasks required to produce the client service and support plan.

Evaluation of teamwork is formative in the sense that evaluation can occur during the *completion step* of each team meeting. This information can then be reviewed during the *orientation step* of the next meeting. Through such methods of ongoing evaluation, the team members can improve the effectiveness of the process, and the outcomes of its planning. Tables 3.2 and 3.3 identify examples of tools that interdisciplinary teams can use in the formative evaluation of group process and task fulfillment.

LEADING AN INTERDISCIPLINARY TEAM

Case managers may or may not be the designated chair or coordinator of an interdisciplinary team. In some models of service delivery, such as hospice care, the case manager is a nurse who also serves as the coordinator of the interdisciplinary team responsible for the development of a hospice care plan (Herzog, 1985). However, in other service situations such as mental health settings, hospitals, and rehabilitation programs the case manager may not be the person who exercises formal authority over the team.

Just because the case manager may lack formal authority does not mean that he or she will exercise no leadership within the interdisciplinary team.

TABLE 3.2 Checklist for the Formative Evaluation of Team Process

YES	NO	
____	____	1. The team allocates time for members to get to know one another on a personal basis.
____	____	2. The team allocates time to orienting members to the goals and objectives of the meeting.
____	____	3. Group norms reinforce cooperation of members rather than competition.
____	____	4. Members are encouraged to share their feelings and perspectives regarding the work of the team.
____	____	5. Members are encouraged to make contributions to the work of the team.
____	____	6. The team encourages participation of the client.
____	____	7. Conflict is openly recognized and dealt with among team members.
____	____	8. There is a mutual understanding of the roles and functions of team members.
____	____	10. Leadership is assigned based on who can best address the particular tasks which must be accomplished during a team meeting.
____	____	11. There is a team member (or members) who encourages participation, relief of tension, active listening, and resolution of conflict.
____	____	12. The size of the team is kept small enough for members to accomplish their work effectively.
____	____	13. During each meeting the team reviews its operating procedures.
____	____	14. Decisions which are important to accomplishing the purpose of the meeting have been made.
____	____	15. Decision-making usually occurs by consensus.
____	____	16. Informal training focusing on effective teamwork usually occurs during a meeting.

Leadership can be defined in the context of an interdisciplinary team as "the equal stake members of the (team) see themselves as having in achieving group goals and group morale" (Kokopeli & Lakey, n.d., p. 11). The implication of this definition is that the case manager uses his or her knowledge of the client's needs and his or her influence within the team to help it achieve the goal of developing a relevant and responsive client service and support plan (Sampson & Marthas, 1981).

The membership of an effective interdisciplinary team will recognize the many leadership assets within the group, and will therefore provide opportunities for all of its members to lead (Bradford, 1976). Although there may be a formally designated team coordinator or chair, each member can exert leadership at one time or another.

TABLE 3.3 Checklist for the Formative Evaluation of Team Product

YES	NO	
———	———	1. The needs of the client serve as the focus of the work of the team.
———	———	2. Members are informed about the agenda prior to the meeting.
———	———	3. The team reviews the agenda at the beginning of each meeting.
———	———	4. Information and resources for accomplishing the purpose of the meeting are adequate.
———	———	5. The length of the meeting is sufficient to accomplish the agenda.
———	———	6. The team has a set of operating procedures that guide each meeting.
———	———	7. Adequate progress is made during each meeting toward the completion of the client service and support plan.
———	———	8. Input from the client is reflected in the plan.
———	———	9. Input from social network members is reflected in the plan.
———	———	10. The team has the appropriate expertise to accomplish its work.
———	———	11. Output of the team is reviewed at the end of each meeting.
———	———	12. Overall, the team works in an efficient manner.
———	———	13. Overall, the team works in an effective manner.

A flexible approach to leadership behavior is critical within interdisciplinary teams because there are two major leadership categories that the team must address, neither of which can be achieved by any one individual. The first category can be labeled "task achievement." This category focuses the case manager on working with the team in achieving its goals. Leadership activities include goal setting, generation of intervention strategies, summarization and synthesis of information and activities, and the coordination of input from all participants. Successful realization of these activities directly relates to the production of a client service and support plan.

The second category can be labeled "team maintenance" (Bradford, 1976). Leadership activities within this category focus on the promotion of group process and cohesion, and include encouraging participation, relieving tension, active listening, and resolving conflict. Execution of these activities enables the team to complete its work successfully.

For the case manager, the exercise of team leadership is an important dimension of the planning function. Leading an interdisciplinary team means that a case manager can engage in either task leadership or maintenance leadership. Leadership within the team can be further strengthened by identifying different participants who work together as co-facilitators of the interdisciplinary team.

INVOLVING CLIENTS AND SOCIAL NETWORK MEMBERS
IN INTERDISCIPLINARY TEAM PROCESS

Client involvement is a benchmark value of case management practice. Case managers involve clients by including them as partners in the identification of their needs and strengths, in the prioritization of their needs, and in the development of a relevant service and support plan (Roberts-DeGennaro, 1987). Underlying these activities is a commitment by the case manager to involving clients in opportunities to make meaningful choices about the fulfillment of their needs (Gardner, 1980).

The client and his needs are the center of all interdisciplinary team activity. In addition, the client participates in the team as an equal member by sharing his perspectives and by making decisions.

Some clients may be wary of becoming involved fully in the work of the interdisciplinary team. Lack of power, the feeling that they may have little to contribute, and having had poor past experiences with human service professionals all can set the stage for a lack of involvement on the part of clients (Gardner, 1980). The case manager, therefore, must be conscious of providing supports that will sustain successful client involvement. These supports can include:

1. Helping the client to identify his desires, perspectives, and positions before the team meeting, and enabling the client to rehearse the expression of these views prior to the interdisciplinary team session.

2. Counseling and supporting the client during the team meeting to assure that he has shared his perspectives, has responded to those issues deliberated by the team, and has introduced issues of personal importance.

3. Debriefing the client after the team meeting to ensure that the case manager obtains feedback from the client about the content, decisions, and outcomes of the meeting.

4. Leading the interdisciplinary team in evaluating the level of involvement of all participants and in identifying ways for encouraging involvement in subsequent meetings.

Involving social network members is also a very important aspect of interdisciplinary team process. During assessment, the case manager will learn about the client's support system, and opportunities for involving social network members in both planning and intervention will emerge. Key social network members such as neighbors, friends, family members, and extended kin can be invited to attend interdisciplinary team sessions. Of course, such involvement is consummated only after the client has identified those individuals whom he wants invited.

Like the client, social network members may require supports for becoming involved. Training and education for effective participation, transportation, and the scheduling of convenient meeting times are some examples of the supports required in order to make team sessions accessible to social network members (Moxley, Raider, & Cohen, 1987).

A NOTE ON INVOLVING ADVOCATES IN INTERDISCIPLINARY TEAM PROCESS

In many situations a case manager will be working with clients who cannot fully represent themselves in the process of planning. In such situations should the case manager serve as the advocate for the client?

The test here is whether the case manager can represent the interests of the client as if they were his own (Wolfensberger & Zauha, 1973). This may not be difficult to achieve when the case manager is seeking services for a client and must negotiate with, pressure, or otherwise influence other service providers to respond to the needs of the client.

Yet, in some situations the case manager may not be the best advocate for the client. In instances where the client wants to refuse certain services or to fulfill his needs in ways with which professionals do not agree, the case manager should reflect on whether he can represent these desires on the part of the client. If the case manager cannot represent the client in such a way, he may want to involve an external client advocate in the process of interdisciplinary decision-making.

Such advocates may be family members, legal guardians, attorneys, or professional advocates from other organizations. Some communities have agencies devoted to protecting the rights of persons with disabilities and may offer the involvement of their professional staff or volunteer lay advocates.

In such situations the case manager may be courting conflict by purposefully including an external advocate in the team process. However, such inclusion may actually enhance the quality of decision-making and provide for better representation of the client. Involvement of external advocates can serve as a ''check and balance'' on the team as it weighs the client's needs with the resources and interests of human service agencies.

CONCLUSION

The development of the client service and support plan is a pivotal function of case management practice. It is a fundamental step toward the fulfillment of client needs because it actually operationalizes how these needs will be addressed. This planning function also sets the stage for the effective monitoring and evaluation of all service delivery and support efforts.

However, before moving on to the functions of monitoring and evaluation let us review how case managers may structure their roles in working directly with clients to address their needs as well as working with the client's environment in order to build social networks and service delivery systems that are more responsive to human needs.

EXERCISES

1. Choose a current client service plan. While reviewing it respond to the following questions: (1) Does the plan clearly identify a workplan and a division of labor among professionals, the client, and social network members?; (2) Does the plan reflect participation by social network members and by the client?; (3) Does the plan serve as a system of accountability and guidance for you?; (4) Are the goals and objectives that are identified within the plan clear enough for you to evaluate?

2. Attempt to rewrite the plan using the form included in Table 3.1. When you complete the plan use the questions above to evaluate it.

3. Make arrangements to participate in an interdisciplinary team as an observer. Evaluate the extent to which the team is effective in specifying its purpose, achieving coordination, in communicating among members, and in the critique of its own functioning.

4. Examine your caseload and identify the clients who you feel would benefit from the involvement of an external advocate. List your reasons for involving an external advocate. Do these reasons suggest guidelines for when to involve an advocate in the deliberations and decisions of an interdisciplinary team?

Chapter 4

The Direct Service Function of Case Management

KEY QUESTIONS

---

1. **Why is self-direction an important outcome of the direct service function of case management?**

2. **What are the four bases of promoting self-direction on the part of clients of case managers?**

3. **What are the three important dimensions of the helping process?**

4. **What are the six direct service roles of case managers?**

5. **How do case managers use each of these roles?**

INTRODUCTION

To what extent should case managers work directly with their clients? A recurring theme within case management—especially within the mental health field—is whether the case manager should serve as a person's primary psychotherapist (Lamb, 1980; Deitchman, 1980). According to Dill (1987), one side of this debate argues for the case manager to integrate both system intervention roles and psychotherapeutic roles (Lamb, 1980) whereas the other emphasizes the need for the case manager to maintain a focus on systems-level work.

The purpose of this chapter is to reframe the direct service function of the case manager. It is not intended to define the direct service function of the case manager as psychotherapeutic work or even as counseling activity. Rather, it is emphasized that the case manager can assume several different direct service roles designed to increase the effectiveness of the case management process itself by enhancing the client's capacities to fulfill his or her own needs. After all, the case management process, as defined in this book, seeks to enhance the client's ability to be autonomous and self-directed.

GOALS OF THE CHAPTER

Explicating a framework of the direct service function of the case manager is the major focus of this chapter. Thus, its goals are to:

1. Discuss the importance of promoting the self-direction of the client toward being able to undertake case management functions and tasks on his own initiative.
2. Present a conceptual framework of the direct service function of case management.
3. Identify and discuss six direct service roles of case managers.

THE IMPORTANCE OF SELF-DIRECTION

Figure 4.1 presents the conceptual framework used to guide the material presented in this chapter. Examination of this framework reveals that the promotion of client self-direction is a major outcome of the direct service function of case managers. Before getting into the actual roles case managers undertake to move the client toward higher levels of self-direction, a brief outline of the importance of this concept is given.

Case managers often work with people who have multiple problems and disabilities. Many of these individuals have experienced mistreatment, rejection, and outright discrimination. Thus, they may have learned to view themselves as lacking power and skills to effect change in their lives. In the words of Seligman (1975), such individuals may have learned to be helpless.

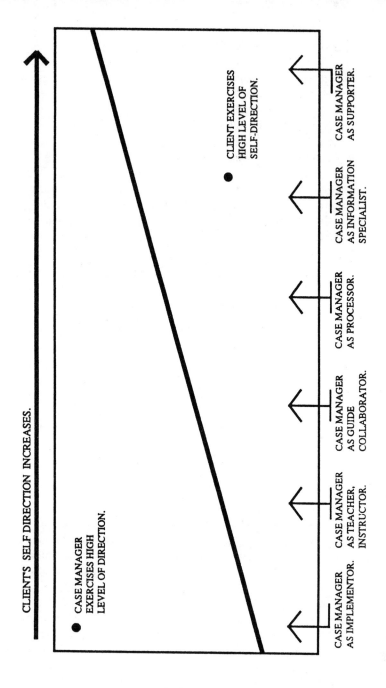

Figure 4.1. Examples of Direct Intervention Roles Available to Case Managers.

Counteracting this ''learned helplessness'' is a major outcome of the direct service function of case management. However, rather than focusing exclusively on the deficits of a client, self-direction is a more positive conception of the potential of the client. Self-direction can be defined as a client's expectancy that he has the capacity to change his situation by using (or acquiring) skills, abilities, and resources to fulfill his own needs.

Self-direction is important for three reasons. First, the attainment of self-direction is culturally congruent since there is so much emphasis on individualism and self-sufficiency within our society. Second, the attainment of self-direction can reduce clients' dependency on professionals and formal services to meet their needs. Finally, by moving towards self-direction the client can realize higher levels of autonomy.

The bases underlying self-direction cut across four areas that must be addressed by both the client and the case manager together. These include:

1. The value base.   Self-direction evolves out of a value base which emphasizes the individualization of the client by the case manager, and the existence of trust between the case manager and the client. Individualization is a cornerstone value of the case management process as we have seen in not only our conceptualization of case management as a human service model but also in how the case manager implements the functions of assessment and planning. Basically, individualization means that the case manager views the client as a person who is unique. That is, as having distinctive feelings, thoughts, experiences, and goals (Compton & Galaway, 1979).

Trust is relevant to the direct service function of case management because it involves the extent to which the case manager has faith in the capacity of the client to move toward autonomy. In other words, the context of promoting self-direction of the client is strengthened if the case manager believes that the client can achieve this goal.

2. Cognitive and attitudinal base.   The existence of trust on part of the case manager raises the contribution of expectancies to achieving self-direction. Critical here is the expectation of growth and development on the part of the client that will result in movement toward more complex behavior, no matter how slowly this process unfolds. These attitudes can operate at several levels and include expectations of growth and change that are held not only by the case manager, but also by the client himself and the significant others who influence the client. Without these expectations operating in the case management situation it is difficult to motivate people to engage in behavior that will ultimately contribute to the realization of self-direction (Maluccio, 1981).

3. Skill base. Trust, expectations, and attitudes establish the context of self-direction. However, the client may require the development of skills to attain this valued end. These can include both cognitive and behavioral skills. Cognitive skills relate to the decision-making process and how the client organizes this process to reach a decision. The value-base of the direct service function identifies autonomy as an important end. To achieve this goal clients (or their advocates) must make decisions for themselves. Identifying preferences and criteria that can be used to evaluate alternatives, and making choices from these alternatives may be an important cognitive skill in supporting the self-direction of a client.

Behavioral skills also can be important to the client's attainment of self-direction. Skills in self-expression, communication, organization, and assertiveness, as well as social skills, are just some of the tools clients may require in order to fulfill their needs.

4. The helping base. The capacity of the case manager to assist the client in moving towards self-direction is influenced by the nature of the helping relationship that exists between these two individuals. The importance of values and expectancies on part of the case manager that contribute to the context of promoting self-direction has been highlighted. The case manager must operationalize these further by building an optimal helping relationship.

Three aspects of the helping relationship are important here. First, the case manager must emphasize accepting and respecting the client. Second, the case manager must be conscious of his or her communication with the client. It is important for the case manager to communicate to each client an understanding of that person's position and feelings about the nature and focus of direct service activities. A third aspect is the achievement of a contractual agreement between the client and the case manager. The contract outlines the work to be undertaken in order to move toward client self-direction, and the supports the case manager will provide in order to assist the client in undertaking this work.

Although self-direction is an important distal goal of case management practice, it must be individualized for each client. People come to case managers with different capacities and abilities. Yet based on the conviction that all people can grow and develop in positive ways, the case manager will design his or her direct service interventions in ways that move clients closer to the goal of self-direction and autonomy no matter how slow or small this movement may be.

SIX DIRECT SERVICE ROLES OF CASE MANAGERS

Figure 4.1 displays the six direct service roles of case managers. Each direct service role varies according to how much the case manager exercises direction and how much self-direction is exercised by the client. In this section each of these roles is explained, followed by a case example that illustrates the use of that role by the case manager.

CASE MANAGER AS IMPLEMENTER

When assuming the role of "implementer," the case manager recognizes that he or she is exercising a high degree of direction over the client. Such a role may appear to be contrary to the desire of the case manager to promote a client's self-direction. However, from my own practice experience as well as in my discussions with other case managers, I have found that this role is usually reserved for working with clients during periods of crisis (Moxley, 1984). It is not unusual for a case manager to make contact with clients who may be experiencing a very disruptive life event and, consequently, who may be immobilized. A crisis occurs for a client when an event overwhelms the person's usual problem-solving methods and leaves him helpless and unable to effectively cope with the situation (Barten, 1971; Dixon, 1979).

Such immobilization calls for direct action from the case manager. A life event such as the loss of housing, the death of a significant other, or the loss of income may precipitate a crisis and create a temporary or episodic situation in which the client cannot cope. This lack of coping becomes the focus of case management intervention, with the "implementer" role becoming important.

In working as an implementer, the case manager makes use of crisis intervention techniques to establish a stable situation for the client. To achieve this, the case manager implements several activities. *Environmental modification* requires the case manager to conduct a rapid assessment of the formal and informal resources available to the client. A rapid review of all need areas and then rapid arrangement of basic resources such as temporary housing, income, and mental health care may be required (Dixon, 1979; Grinnell, Kyte, & Bostwick, 1981).

The use of the implementer role in resolving a crisis situation also requires the case manager to engage in the provision of *psychological support*. According to Dixon (1979), a crisis situation will leave the client in a weakened state in which he is likely to experience deep feelings of depression, anxiety, loneliness, and failure. The case manager responds by interacting with the person on a face-to-face basis providing assurance, reinforcement of the person's self-esteem, and the encouragement of positive feelings and self-expression (Dixon, 1979). Useful techniques for providing psychological support include active listening, expression of empathy, ventilation, clarification, and the provision of advice. As for the final technique, it is not unusual for the case manager to instruct the client (or a third party) directly in what to do. Alternatively, it is not unusual for the case manager to take direct action for clients when they are so immobilized that their self-direction is limited.

A third approach to working with a client in crisis involves the provision of *cognitive restoration*. Emotionality, confusion, and impeded thought are salient characteristics of a crisis state (Dixon, 1979). The provision of support will reduce the client's emotionality thereby permitting opportunities for the person to begin to engage in problem-solving. By helping the person understand what caused the crisis and by clarifying major aspects of the problem, the case manager begins to restore the client's cognitive balance.

As the person's living situation is stabilized and as the case manager works to lower the emotionality of the situation, the person can begin to assume more responsibility for his situation. When this is achieved, the case manager can then move out of the role of implementer.

> Case vignette.   Joe Myers met his client, Mr. Jacobs, for the first time when he was admitted to a short-term crisis house operated by a mental health center. Mr. Jacobs had been admitted to the crisis house after being evicted from his apartment by his landlord. It was obvious to Joe that his client was very debilitated. Mr. Jacobs had been living on the street for about five days. Recognizing that Mr. Jacobs was very confused and anxious about the situation, he provided enriched psychological support as a means of lowering the emotionality of his client. After about one hour, Mr. Jacobs was able to talk about the eviction and the factors that caused it. Once Mr. Jacobs was stable, Joe began work on an alternative housing arrangement and to arrange for the client to stay with a close friend until he could move to a new household. Within 72 hours Mr. Jacobs had moved to his friend's house and had appointments to look at two new apartments. The client then began work with the case manager on fulfilling his other needs.

CASE MANAGER AS TEACHER/INSTRUCTOR

It is not unusual for a case manager to work directly with clients in developing skills which are useful to them in becoming their own case managers and in subsequently fulfilling their own needs. One axiom of case management may be to teach "clients how to fish rather than catching fish for them." Assuming the role of teacher or instructor may be a strategy that a case manager undertakes in moving a client closer to autonomy.

The teaching of independent living skills has gained currency within the human services. Making use of research from behavioral and social learning theories, practitioners have developed skill acquisition and skill building technologies for a number of different independent living needs and several different target populations (Bellack & Hersen, 1979; Goldstein, 1981; Goldstein, Sprafkin, Gershaw, & Klein, 1980). Schutz, Vogelsberg, and Rusch (1980) demonstrated that behavioral approaches can be used to teach mentally retarded persons the skills of community mobility, self-care, money management, telephone use, leisure and recreation, and sustaining employment.

The implication here is that case managers have a technology available to them to work directly with their clients in the acquisition of skills necessary to fulfilling their needs. In operationalizing the role of teacher, case managers can make use of structured learning in helping their clients acquire identified skills.

In teaching their client skills, case managers make use of five specific steps in the instructional process (Goldstein et al., 1980). These include the following:

1. Identification of the skill.   The case manager works with the client in identifying the skills which will be the focus of teaching. These may involve learning interpersonal skills, locating an apartment, locating employment, making friends, or negotiating benefits at the social service department.

2. Modeling.   The case manager then models the desired skills so that they can be imitated by the client. This may involve breaking down complex skills into discrete behaviors so that the client can readily observe those behaviors which are important to successful execution of the skill. Effective modeling will occur if the case manager demonstrates skills in a clear and detailed manner, in the order from least difficult to most difficult, and with enough repetition to make overlearning a likely outcome (Goldstein et al., 1980).

3. Role playing.   The case manager encourages the client to engage in the behavior that has been demonstrated. Role playing allows the client to practice the behavior on a repeated basis and within a safe environment. Concern for failure should be eliminated; and the client should have many

opportunities to practice. The effects of role playing are enhanced if the person freely chooses to be involved, if the person is committed to learning the skill, and if the person receives reward and approval for engaging in the behavior (Goldstein et al., 1980).

4. Performance feedback.   Reinforcement is necessary to skill acquisition and to the effectiveness of role playing. Three types of reinforcers can be used by the case manager to encourage skill acquisition. These are material reinforcement (food or money), social reinforcement (approval from others), and self-reinforcement (one's positive evaluation of one's own behavior). Whichever reinforcer is used, it is important for the case manager to deliver it as soon as possible after the demonstration of the desired behavior (Sundel & Sundel, 1975).

5. Transfer of training.   It is important for the case manager and the client to make arrangements for the client to practice and use the acquired skills in real-life settings. Thus, the client has opportunities to transfer the skill learned in a secure training setting to the actual settings in which it will be used.

The following vignette demonstrates how the case manager may assume a teaching role vis-à-vis the client.

Case vignette.   Mr. Smith is a young man who has had a major psychiatric problem for much of his life. He has worked with one case manager for two years now but has recently decided to work on his own behalf in negotiating income and vocational benefits. Mr. Smith and the case manager agree that this will provide him with an opportunity to move toward more independence. One system with which Mr. Smith wants to negotiate for additional benefits is the state vocational rehabilitation office. In particular, he wants this office to support a training experience for him. Mr. Smith works with his case manager in identifying the skills he needs for negotiating with the state counselor. They break these skills down, and the case manager models each one. Mr. Smith then role-plays the negotiation skills he will use while the case manager reinforces his successful execution with verbal praise. After several teaching sessions, the case manager asks a friend who is a state counselor to meet with Mr. Smith in a simulated session of the negotiation. This "transfer of training" allows Mr. Smith to practice his negotiation skills in a real-life situation. After two of these sessions, Mr. Smith felt that he was ready to make an appointment with a counselor from the state office of vocational rehabilitation.

The role of teacher and instructor is a powerful one for the case manager. Armed with an effective technology, the case manager can individualize the process of teaching clients basic living skills as well as more complex social, interpersonal, and decision-making skills. However, this role involves a high degree of case management direction. Although the product of the training may be increased self-direction on the part of the client, the process of teaching and instruction is directed by the case manager.

CASE MANAGER AS GUIDE/COLLABORATOR

In executing their direct service role of guide and collaborator, the case manager works with the client in identifying the human service resources the client requires to fulfill his needs, and then guides the client through the process of obtaining these services and supports. This process is less intrusive than either directly implementing a plan of action or teaching skills directly to the client. Rather, in this role the case manager undertakes the following tasks:

1. The case manager meets with the client on a face-to-face basis to discuss the services and supports that are required to fulfill the client's needs.
2. The case manager and the client collaborate in the identification of appropriate services and supports required by the client.
3. The case manager and the client schedule follow-up meetings with the professionals and social network members whose services and supports are needed by the client.
4. The case manager and the client meet other professionals and social network members to discuss the client's situation and to negotiate the provision of the services and supports.

There are several reasons why this role is an important one for the case manager. First, the case manager forms a collaborative relationship with the client in which the latter is directly involved in the process of obtaining services and supports. Consequently, it builds and/or strengthens the client's self-direction. Second, successful execution of the role encourages the client to develop problem-solving skills. The client can learn how to define his needs, examine alternative services and supports to fulfill these needs, and then link with the providers who can meet these needs. Finally, the case manager can model ways for the client to work with providers. During the negotiation process the client remains with the case manager and can observe the case manager in "action." These opportunities for observation can help clients learn more about the skills and abilities they require to successfully meet their needs.

Case vignette.   Linda Clark, a case manager for the local mental health center, has worked with Sally Freedman for close to a year. Ms. Freedman has had problems with severe depression. At the beginning of her treatment at the mental health center, she was very dependent on her case manager to help her meet her needs. Currently, Ms. Freedman is doing well and is moving quickly toward being self-directed and independent. Linda is working with her client as a guide and collaborator. Recently, Ms. Freedman and the case manager met and identified postsecondary education in computer programming as a highly desirable opportunity to help Ms. Freedman prepare for a vocation. The client and case manager identified issues involving financial aid, an appropriate educational setting, transportation, and housing. Linda used her knowledge of local educational and vocational resources to guide Ms. Freedman through the process of identifying appropriate educational opportunities. During the meeting, Ms. Freedman then called a counselor at the local community college to discuss enrollment. The plan called for Linda to accompany Ms. Freedman to this meeting and to participate in the discussion of the possible enrollment of her client in a computer training curriculum.

CASE MANAGER AS PROCESSOR

Successful use of the role of processor by case managers requires them to understand whether their clients are prepared to act with a high level of self-direction. Case managers are available to clients to help them identify alternatives for meeting their needs and to help them choose the appropriate service and support that may be of assistance to them. Through the use of this role, case managers not only help the client move through a process of problem-solving but also make available to the client their expert knowledge of the resources available within the community. The latter aspect of this role is labeled as technical assistance. However, it is up to the client to take autonomous action in linking with identified resources.

Technical assistance is a viable aspect of the processor role. Many case managers have considerable information and knowledge about community resources and what is required to access these resources. In providing technical assistance, the case manager makes this knowledge base available to the client. The client, therefore, has a resource of knowledge, expertise, and experience from which he can draw in order to fulfill his or her needs.

Case vignette.   Pat Williams is a case manager working at an independent living center located in an inner city neighborhood. The center specializes in supporting the independent living of persons with severe physical disabilities. Pat works with a number of clients who have special needs regarding transportation, housing, and recreation. For the most part, his clients are well-motivated and able to respond to these special needs. However, he has developed a reputation for being quite knowledgeable of housing resources within the community, especially housing which is physically accessible to persons who use wheelchairs. Members of the independent living center who are looking for housing often drop in to see Pat. They discuss their housing needs and review with the case manager the desirable attributes of the housing which they are seeking. Very often Pat is able to identify several housing alternatives that the members can subsequently investigate on their own initiative. It also is not unusual for some members to be unclear about their housing needs. In these cases, Pat explores their needs and then helps them to identify appropriate options that they can then investigate on their own.

CASE MANAGER AS INFORMATION SPECIALIST

This role evolves out of case managers' specialized knowledge of human services, benefit systems, and opportunities available to their clients within the community. This information base is often formalized by case managers by being transformed into resource data bases. Such data bases may take the form of card catalogues, resource books, pamphlets, or flyers listing resources such as housing or computer data bases, within a specific area.

The case manager becomes an information specialist by virtue of developing, using, maintaining, and updating these information systems, and by providing clients with opportunities to make use of them. As an information specialist the case manager may orient clients as to the use of the information system and then show them how to actually use it to identify community resources, benefits, or services.

As in the processor role, the case manager places an emphasis on serving as a technical agent who enables clients to build their knowledge about fulfilling particular needs. In the role of information specialist, the case manager is not very intrusive. Rather, the case manager is concerned about whether clients have sufficient information to fulfill their needs through the best resources available. It is then up to the clients themselves to follow through on accessing the identified resources.

Case vignette.   During his tenure as a case manager at the independent living center, Pat Williams has developed a comprehensive inventory of resources that support independent living on part of people with severe physical disabilities. This system began as a small booklet that mainly presented information about available housing within the community. However, as demand for information grew among the members of the independent living center, Pat modified the system so that profiles of housing, educational, recreational, employment, and other resources were maintained on index cards.

Finally, Pat obtained a small foundation grant to convert this card system into an automated data base that operates out of a personal computer. The foundation grant underwrote the purchase of four personal computers.

Pat is now able to respond to the information needs of many of his clients. He holds a monthly workshop on how to use the computer systems. Clients are encouraged to make use of the computer stations on their own. One of Pat's major tasks is to update the resource data base periodically.

CASE MANAGER AS SUPPORTER

The case manager operationalizes the role of supporter when the client is able to exercise a high level of self-direction. From this author's perspective this role is a culmination of the previous ones and requires the client to engage in self-advocacy. The latter concept refers to the ability of clients to advance their own cause by being able to locate and access the resources that they need to fulfill their needs. Case managers who define their role as promoting the self-direction of a client will move logically toward the promotion of self-advocacy since it means that clients will gain the capacities to act on their own behalf. Such clients become less dependent on the case manager.

The capacity to act on one's own behalf evolves out of clients' acquiring several attributes that will underwrite their ability to care for themselves. One important capacity is that of knowledge. Clients gain knowledge of their own needs and the resources available to meet those needs. A second important area is that of skills. For example, the client develops problem-solving skills which support effective decision-making. In addition, skills relevant to solving crises and negotiating with service providers are important here. Self-perception is a third important area. Perceiving oneself as being able to effect change in one's situation and to expect that one can grow and develop are important qualities that influence the realization of self-advocacy.

The essence of the role of supporter is that the case manager supports the self-advocacy of the client and the movement of the client toward higher levels of self-direction. How does the case manager actualize this role? One way is for the case manager to be available to clients in order to help them cope with the problems that may evolve out of the exercise of self-advocacy. Clients may confront bureaucrats who are intransigent in responding to their needs. This can result in feelings of frustration and anger. The case manager can be available to listen to these feelings and to serve as a sounding board.

Another way for the case manager to actualize this role is by serving as an enabler. This term is not used in the traditional sense of enabling the client to obtain required services. Rather it means that the case manager enables clients to reach higher levels of appeal in order to make their needs known to an agency. For example, if a client is not able to obtain a service from a lower level official, the case manager may use his or her influence to help the client access an administrator at a higher level of the organization through whom the client can appeal his request. Such activity on the part of the case manager may create conflict. Yet, this action may create a positive outcome for the client and reinforce the client's feelings of efficacy—that, indeed, he can try to influence his situation in a positive way.

Finally, the case manager may actualize the role of supporter by engaging in sustaining activities. The realities of self-advocacy may weigh heavily on the client. It is not unusual for frustration, anger, feelings of defeat, and loss of motivation to well up in a client. The response of the case manager is to sustain the client by imparting hope, by providing praise for his or her efforts, by listening closely to his or her concerns and feelings, and by identifying the small successes and progress the client has made in advancing his or her interests. Thus, empathy, enabling, and sustaining become major strategies the case manager employs in supporting the self-advocacy of a client.

CONCLUSION

This chapter has explored a number of ways a case manager can work with clients in promoting their self-direction. The direct service function provides a means of building and strengthening the self-care capacities of a client. By not operationalizing this function the case manager loses opportunities to promote the independence of his or her clientele.

However, the direct service function is not the only means of intervention available to a case manager. Environmental intervention also is an important component of case management. Therefore, human service delivery systems and social networks are legitimate targets of the intervention armamentarium of case managers.

EXERCISES

1. Identify a client for whom you are currently providing case management services. Using the six direct service roles identified in this chapter, indicate how you can promote the self-direction of this client.

2. Select a skill that is important to the client in learning how to respond to his or her own needs. Write down the steps you will undertake to help the client learn this skill.

3. Identify a client who has recently experienced a crisis. How did you work with this client in resolving this crisis? Were your activities consistent with the framework presented in this chapter? If so, how were your activities consistent? If not, how were your activities different?

4. Select a client from your current caseload. How can you promote the self-advocacy of this client? How will you support the client's self-advocacy?

Chapter 5

The Indirect Service Function of Case Management

KEY QUESTIONS

1. What is the role of indirect services in case management practice?
2. What are six indirect service strategies used by case managers?
3. How do case managers use each of these strategies?
4. How does the case manager make use of personal and professional influence in attempting to organize and obtain services for a client?
5. How does the case manager use pressure or conflict-laden strategies to organize and obtain services for a client?

INTRODUCTION

As identified in Chapter 1, the indirect service function involves the case manager in changing the behavior or performance of a system on behalf of a client. The case manager, therefore, makes use of activities and interventions which are implemented with systems external to the client as a means of operationalizing the service plan, as a means of building the capacities of these systems to respond to the needs of clients, and to provide the client with access to resources (Steinberg & Carter, 1983).

The case manager using the indirect service function is sensitive to four aspects of this function. One aspect is *systemic change* at an organizational level or at the level of human service delivery networks. To realize such change the case manager may work with an agency in creating new resources or services, in serving clients who previously were not seen as appropriate by the agency, or even in influencing the modification of—or development of new—organizational goals or policies (Pierce, 1984; Rothman, Erlich, & Teresa, 1981). The resulting systemic change may be large or small—incremental or revolutionary. To accomplish this change, however, the "tool kit" of the case manager must contain techniques and strategies for realizing change in the environment of the client (Maluccio, 1981).

As implied above, another aspect of the indirect service function is *environmental intervention*. Much of the work of a case manager will be done apart from the client. The case manager is conscious of a client's needs, and he or she will use specific techniques to effect change in the client's environment. So, if systemic change is to be a viable outcome of case management practice the vehicle for realizing this goal is environmental intervention. It is imperative here that the case manager know how to assess the client's environment and to intervene in this environment with the goal of fulfilling the needs of the client.

Evolving out of systemic change and environmental intervention is a third aspect of the indirect service function: *capacity-building*. Basically, this term means that in doing the work of case management the case manager is conscious of strengthening the network of community resources so that it will be responsive to other clients in the future (Steinberg & Carter, 1983). An encounter between an agency and a case manager presents a "critical opportunity" for improving the delivery of services to clients. For example, successfully influencing a family service agency to serve a person with severe mental illness can open up such services for other clients experiencing similar problems.

Finally, by seeking to improve the capacities of human services case managers can influence the development and delivery of resources within their communities. A major concern of case managers is the identification and organization of *resources that meet the needs of their clients*. By engaging in a change agentry role, and by viewing each encounter with service providers as an opportunity for effecting systemic change, the case manager can influence the development of new resources and programs (Schaefer, 1987).

The purpose of this chapter is to identify and discuss strategies that can be used by case managers in implementing the indirect service function. Some of these strategies can be used alone or in combination with others. Some rely on influence techniques like negotiation and bargaining, whereas others may require the case manager to make use of conflict. Nonetheless they are all part of the case manager's "tool kit" and can be used in realizing the fulfillment of client needs.

GOALS OF THE CHAPTER

Outlining indirect service strategies is the major focus of this chapter. The three primary goals are to:

1. Identify the importance of the indirect service function of case management practice.
2. Identify and discuss six indirect service strategies.
3. Identify some useful tools for executing the indirect service function.

SIX INDIRECT SERVICE STRATEGIES OF CASE MANAGERS

The indirect service strategies employed by case managers enable them to obtain services and resources for clients as well as to influence the capacities of these services and resources to respond to client needs. *Brokering* and *linkage* are two strategies that enable clients to obtain formal human services. *Advocacy* is a useful strategy for obtaining services and for increasing the availability and accessibility of services. *Coordination* is used by the case manager to assure that service providers work together in responding to client needs effectively. *Social network intervention* is used to enhance the provision of resources by the client's social support system. Finally, *technical assistance and consultation* is a strategy used by the case manager in working directly with either formal human service providers or social network members. The goal of this strategy is to enhance the responsiveness of these actors to the needs of the client.

Each of these strategies is discussed below, and its relevance to case management is highlighted. Before moving on to our discussion of these strategies it is important to emphasize that their use follows from the client's service and support plan. This plan identifies the needs of the client and how these needs will be met by the case manager, members of the interdisciplinary team, other human service providers, and by social network members. Thus, the case manager is acutely aware that the indirect service function is directed ultimately by the overall case management plan. The criterion for evaluating the effectiveness of the indirect service function lies in whether the appropriate intervention activities were undertaken, and whether these interventions led to the fulfillment of client needs.

BROKERING SERVICES TO MEET CLIENT NEEDS

Brokering involves the case manager in selecting appropriate agencies or community resources which can deliver the services identified in the client service and support plan. This indirect service strategy is used by the case manager to connect a client to a resource that can appropriately and adequately address the needs of that client.

Why is brokering an important intervention strategy? As noted in Chapter 1, most human service delivery systems are complex and lay people often have inadequate knowledge and information about available services. Alternatively, the information they possess about a community resource may be inaccurate or wrong. In addition, service providers may be unaware of exactly who is in need of services. This is especially true of agencies that do not engage in extensive outreach or awareness building within their communities.

The case manager, therefore, performs the role of broker in order to operationalize the client service and support plan by connecting a client with a community agency or other type of resource (Hepworth & Larsen, 1982). Successful use of this intervention strategy requires a number of skills on part of the case manager.

Effective brokering depends on the case manager's knowledge of the human service delivery system within a particular community. This knowledge is gained and enhanced through the development of resource inventories which are often products of the case management assessment process. By obtaining in-depth information about these resources, the case manager gains the intimate knowledge essential to effective brokering of services. This knowledge includes:

1. The availability, adequacy, appropriateness, acceptability, and accessibility of services. These dimensions are discussed in Chapter 2.
2. Eligibility criteria guiding receipt of services and whether these are need-based (i.e., the client has certain unfulfilled needs), diagnostic-based (i.e., the client must have a certain diagnosis), or means-tested (i.e., the person must meet certain income or resource criteria).
3. The quality of the service as indicated by past provision of services to other clients, by client feedback obtained through evaluation studies, and by accreditation by national commissions such as the Joint Commission of Accredita-

tion of Health Care Organizations and the Commission on the Accreditation of Rehabilitation Facilities.

4. The competence of service providers to address the particular needs or problems of a client. A particular agency may have strong skills in working with a certain type of client. For example, one agency may have strong competence in addressing severe behavior disorders.

5. The motivation of service providers to respond to a particular client. Through their work as brokers of services and resources, case managers become aware of agencies that are motivated or not motivated to respond to client needs. Knowledge of agency reputations will assist the case manager in identifying an appropriate community resource.

6. The service domain of the agency. Some agencies offer comprehensive services which can cover many of the need areas of clients; others offer specialized services within a narrow range. In some situations, case managers can refer to one agency as a means of getting several needs of a client addressed simultaneously, whereas in other cases case managers refer to an agency that provides a single, specialized service.

Another factor influencing effective brokering is the case manager's liaison experience with other agencies. Through personal contacts with agencies and their staffs the case manager builds relationships that over time form a "professional network" (Curtis, 1973, 1974; Erickson, 1975). This network can be used to broker services. It provides a means by which case managers can interact with service providers about specific clients and their needs, and the appropriateness of the agency's services to these clients. Also, through liaison relationships the case manager can include other service providers as members of the interdisciplinary team that constructs the client service and support plan. An outcome of this work is that brokering of services actually begins while a client's services and supports are being planned.

Finally, it is important to point out that case managers can access other agencies through the professional networks of their colleagues. By working with other case managers in staffing cases, developing joint information systems, and sharing "inside" information about the effectiveness, motivation, and quality of other services, case managers can increase their fund of knowledge about community service delivery systems.

Table 5.1 provides an overview of brokering.

LINKING CLIENTS TO SERVICES AND RESOURCES

Brokering involves the identification and organization of community services and resources designed to meet the needs of a client. Linkage is a

TABLE 5.1   An Overview of Brokering

GOAL OF STRATEGY
To identify and select agencies that have services relevant to a client's needs

KEY ELEMENTS OF STRATEGY
1. Case manager's knowledge of service delivery network including knowledge of:
   —Eligibility criteria
   —Quality of service
   —Competence of service providers
   —Motivation of service providers
   —Service domain of agencies
2. Case manager's own professional network and networks of colleagues

---

strategy used by case managers to connect the client to the service in order to assure utilization. One of the principal means of linkage is referral (Hepworth & Larsen, 1982; O'Neil,1984; Weissman, 1976).

Effective referral is a complex process that involves the case manager in conducting mediation work between the client and the identified agency or resource. In working with the client, the case manager must be aware of possible fears, misconceptions, and misunderstandings of the agency or resource to which he or she is being referred (Hepworth & Larsen, 1982). Thus, in linking a client to a referral source the case manager may want to operationalize the following activities:

1. Clearly identify to the client (and/or advocate) those needs in the client service and support plan that require referral to another agency or community resource.

2. Enhance the client's knowledge of the agency or resource so the client understands the need for referral and what can be achieved through the referral. It is important for the case manager to assess and understand the clients's feelings, concerns, apprehensiveness, and preferences regarding the referral.

3. Involve the client as much as possible in selecting the referral agency. If at all possible, present the client with several alternatives so that he or she can act on his or her preferences.

4. Jointly assess with the client the match between the client's needs and the services provided by the agency. Incorporated here should be information obtained through the brokering process and the resource inventory process. Thus, the client, his or her representative, and the case manager can examine information pertaining to eligibility policies, quality of services, competence of

service providers, motivation of service providers, and the service domain of the agency.

5. Identify client constraints and problems in accessing the service, particularly issues pertaining to location of the service, transportation, hours of operations, and the availability of ancillary services such as child care (O'Neill, 1984).

6. Arrange to have a social network member accompany the client if he or she is apprehensive about using the service (Weissman, 1976).

Another important consideration in realizing successful referrals is the preparation of the agency or resource to accept the client. By focusing only on the client's role in the referral process, the case manager may set up a situation that will fail. But by focusing on both sides of the "referral equation"—the client and the agency—the case manager will increase the probability of a successful referral.

The first major step in assuring agency acceptance of the referral is to ascertain whether the agency has the appropriate services, competence, and motivation to work with the client. By failing to ascertain these the case manager cannot be confident that the referral will be accepted.

A second major step involves the transmission of essential information regarding client needs. The case manager follows appropriate confidentiality procedures by counseling the client in informed consent, and by obtaining a release of information. It is important for agency representatives to understand the purpose of the referral, the needs of the client that will be addressed by the agency, and how these needs fit into the overall client service and support plan. Relevant assessment information can be shared with the agency, and this may enable the agency to limit its initial assessment and diagnostic activities thereby allowing for a more expedient delivery of services.

A third major step involves the case manager in working with the agency to resolve barriers or problems that may arise when serving the client. The case manager is aware of the problems that may arise from such factors as lack of transportation, limited hours of operation, lack of needed ancillary services, and a location that may be inaccessible to the client. If the agency can resolve some of these barriers, this is an indicator that the referral may be appropriate. If these problems cannot be resolved this may be an indication of the need to identify another community resource.

What is the mechanism by which the case manager implements these steps? The case manager's use of a *linkage meeting* provides a forum for the realization of a successful referral. The linkage meeting involves the case manager, the client and his or her representative, and agency intake personnel in a face-to-face conference. During this conference the objective of the referral is identified, the required forms identified and perhaps completed, essential information identified and perhaps transmitted to the receiving agency, and potential accessibility barriers and problems identified and resolved. The linkage meeting, therefore, is a structure for the management of the referral process. Also, it can foreshadow subsequent meetings which can focus on coordination, monitoring, and evaluation of the services provided by the agency.

A final basic requirement of linkage is a monitoring system put in place by the case manager. Referral of a client to an agency does not necessarily mean that either the client or the agency will follow through with the services. It is crucial, therefore, for the case manager to monitor the use and delivery of the identified service.

Monitoring of referrals need not be an elaborate or complicated process. Consistent and well-timed telephone calls to the client or to the service provider can alert the case manager to problems of utilization and delivery. In addition, the case manager can ask for periodic correspondence from the service provider with the purpose of providing an "update" of service delivery and utilization. A third alternative is to schedule and implement periodic linkage meetings to review the use and delivery of services. Finally, the case manager, in some cases, will have the authority to audit case records. The case manager then can examine a particular case record to ascertain whether the service is being used and whether it is being delivered in an appropriate manner.

It is important to point out that the purpose of monitoring is not to audit either the client or the service provider. The case manager should explain to both client and service provider that he or she is concerned about whether the referral is appropriate and effective. Thus, if the client is not making use of the service or if the agency is not providing the service, this indicates that the case management process is breaking down and that the needs of the client are not being addressed. In a sense, therefore, monitoring is a means of accountability for the case manager in assuring that the overall process of client need fulfillment stays on the correct path.

In some cases, the case manager may not work extensively with an agency in the linkage process. As emphasized in the previous chapter, linkage may be undertaken as a self-directed activity of the client, or by members of the client's social network. In such situations, the case manager can enhance the skills of clients and social network members in linkage activities through role plays, behavioral rehearsal, and through educational meetings about available community resources. The direct service roles of teacher, guide/collaborator, processor, information specialist, and supporter are relevant here.

Linkage activities are summarized in Table 5.2.

COORDINATING CLIENT SERVICE DELIVERY

As emphasized in previous chapters, the case manager is responsible for the management of a complex process of client service delivery. One indirect service function of importance, therefore, is that of service coordination at the client-level.

The aim of service coordination is to assure that services are being implemented in harmonious and compatible ways by the human service providers and social network members who have been organized by the case manager to respond to client needs. The case manager is concerned about (1) assuring that all actors are attempting to achieve compatible service delivery goals, (2) assuring that the service delivery plan is being implemented according to its design, and (3) assuring that actors are communicating about their service and support activities on a regular basis. The case manager working as a coordinator facilitates the work of the client support network (Egan, 1985) by organizing and maintaining a structure to accomplish the goals of the client service and support plan (Havelock, 1973).

There are a number of barriers to accomplishing effective coordination of client services and supports. Client coordination may be difficult because the agencies involved in the effort may perceive a lack of shared interests (Zald, 1979). In addition, they may feel that they are in competition over access to the very clients around which the case manager is asking them to cooperate (Apolloni & Cooke, 1984). An absence of shared interests and perceived competition raises the problem of turfmanship (Rossi, Gilmartin, & Dayton, 1982). Protecting turf may mean that agencies are attempting to protect their power and independence.

Coordination of client service delivery turns on the important role of the case manager as an organizational boundary-spanner. In Chapter 1 this role was identified as a critical element of case management practice. It requires the case manager to move across the boundaries of many organizations in order to negotiate the transaction of resources on behalf of the client. Keeping in mind this boundary-spanning role will enable the case manager to find solutions to barriers that may block effective service coordination. In coordinating client service delivery the aim of the case manager is to motivate members of the client support network to perceive an interdependence and

TABLE 5.2   An Overview of Linkage

GOAL OF STRATEGY
To connect the client to specific agency services

KEY ELEMENTS OF STRATEGY
1. Following criteria of effective referral.
2. Transmission of essential client information to relevant agencies.
3. Resolution of barriers or problems in serving client.
4. Use of linkage meeting as a primary mechanism of linkage.
5. Importance of developing monitoring system:
    —Consistent telephone calls
    —Periodic correspondence from service providers
    —Periodic linkage meetings
    —Periodic review of clients records

---

a joint mission in addressing client needs. The case manager can use several tactics in encouraging coordination. These include:

1. Emphasizing the needs of the client.   Rossi, Gilmartin, and Dayton (1982) indicate that agencies are more willing to coordinate their efforts when they know they are responding to the immediate needs of clients. It is important, therefore, to place the service coordination effort in the context of client needs.

2. Framing the coordination effort as an ad hoc process.   The case manager can argue that the coordination of client services across agencies is neither binding nor permanent. It exists for the time it takes to address and fulfill the needs of a specific client (Zald, 1979). In addition, the coordination effort does not require the agency to relinquish any power.

3. Agreeing on what is to be coordinated.   Organization and maintenance of an interagency effort to serve a client requires agreement on what is to be coordinated. The case manager may want to develop an informal contract among agency representatives that specifies what is to be coordinated on behalf of the client. The case manager can identify (1) sharing of information, (2) adherence to a common treatment plan across several agencies, (3) exchange of consultation between agencies, and (4) collaboration of agency professionals in serving the client. The contract should be informal, target specific activities, and specify timelines.

4. Identifying benefits of coordination.   The case manager must be conscious of indicating the rewards to agencies for coordinating their efforts. One salient reward is the added information the agency obtains about clients and how to respond to their needs. Another reward is the "goodwill" the

agency obtains within the community and among other agencies for participating in client coordination efforts. A third reward is the potential knowledge the agency gains of other community resources and services. A final reward is the shared responsibility for a particular client. This reward is important when an agency deals with a client whose needs may require expensive, consistent, and long-term interventions.

The case manager articulates the process of client service coordination through four types of mechanisms. These are outlined below:

1. Information exchange and monitoring mechanisms. These mechanisms are used by the case manager to encourage the exchange of information among members of the client support network. One approach is the case coordination conference. These are periodic meetings convened by the case manager so that members of the client support network can exchange information and be kept informed about the development of new client needs, or the fulfillment of current needs. A second approach is the maintenance of a common recording format or information system that can be disseminated among members of the client support network. Such reports, records, or memoranda can include diagnostic information, assessment data, progress reports, and critical incident reports.

2. Capacity-building mechanisms. These mechanisms are used by the case manager to encourage the development of competencies and skills relevant to work with the client or a class of clients. Case consultation is one approach. The case manager can identify expertise in the community, in universities, or among members of the client support network to consult with providers on specific client needs or problems. Joint training is another capacity-building mechanism. The case manager can arrange for experiential training of the entire team. This training can address innovative or state-of-the-art methods of working with the identified client.

3. Adaptation mechanisms. These mechanisms are designed by the case manager to adapt to changes in client needs, in the social network of the client, or in the human service delivery network. Specific mechanisms include (1) milestone conferencing in which the case manager convenes the members of the client support network to identify and discuss new goals after the client has achieved previous ones, (2) transitional conferencing in which the case manager convenes the members of the client support network to plan for the client's movement to a new environment, program, or new phase of treatment, and (3) crisis conferencing in which the case manager convenes the members of the client support network to respond to significant events that have emerged suddenly in the client's life.

4. Networking mechanisms. These are mechanisms used by the case manager to enhance or maintain the functioning of the client support network. They can include (1) third party consultation to reduce conflict within the network, (2) educational sessions to increase the understanding of network members about the services offered by specific agencies, (3) development of procedures for promoting the efficient and effective work of the network, and (4) informal activities that increase the interpersonal cohesiveness of the network such as lunch meetings, opportunities to gain personal knowledge of individual network members, and other opportunities for social interaction.

In implementing and realizing effective client service coordination, the case manager may engage in a considerable amount of community organization. As noted in Chapter 1, an argument for the creation of case management systems is the high level of fragmentation of human services that exists in many of our communities. The case manager who makes use of service coordination mechanisms attempts to offset such fragmentation for specific clients by organizing and maintaining a network that not only coordinates its goal attainment efforts, but also changes these efforts as a client's needs or circumstances change.

Table 5.3 summarizes service coordination activities.

ADVOCATING FOR CLIENTS

Up to this point the discussion of the indirect service function has assumed that human service agencies identified by the case manager are willing to respond to the needs of a client. This may not be the case. The identified agency may feel that the client is unattractive, and therefore deny services. Alternatively, the agency may argue that the client "does not fit into" the types of services it offers. Or, the agency may argue that the client does not behave appropriately, and therefore cannot benefit from the services offered by the agency.

Certainly there is an entire universe of reasons that an agency might invoke in order not to serve a client. If the service is appropriate, however, and will contribute to the well-being of the client, the case manager must be willing to confront the agency and seek responsiveness of that agency to the client. Siporin (1975) identifies this activity as "case advocacy." It involves the case manager in identifying to a community, a social welfare agency, or a welfare system the unmet service needs of a client or a group of clients. Through advocacy activities the case manager attempts to correct an injustice that evolves out of the denial of services. Thus, case ad-

TABLE 5.3   An Overview of Service Coordination

GOAL OF STRATEGY
To implement client services in harmonious and compatible ways
within context of an interagency network

ELEMENTS OF STRATEGY
1. Reduction of barriers to service coordination:
   —Lack of shared interests
   —Perceived competition for clients
   —Turfmanship
2. Use of tactics to encourage coordination:
   —Appeal to client needs
   —Frame coordination as ad hoc
   —Agree on what is to be coordinated and employ informal contracts
   —Identify benefits of coordination
3. Implement coordination mechanisms:
   —Information exchange and monitoring mechanisms
   —Capacity-building mechanisms
   —Adaptation mechanisms
   —Networking mechanisms

---

vocacy is an appropriate intervention strategy when a human service agency is rigid and unwilling to meet the needs of an identified client or group of clients (Johnson & Rubin, 1983).

Sosin and Caulum (1983) argue that advocacy involves the use of influence or confrontation techniques to get an individual or group to make a decision regarding the welfare of a third party who is in a less powerful position than the decision maker. Using this definition of advocacy, the case manager may be in a position of "representing" to an agency the interests of a client who has less power than agency decision makers. The successful outcome of advocacy realized by the case manager is the access of the client to agency resources and services. Two important questions are raised here. First, what is the "powerbase" of the case manager? Second, what tactics does the case manager use in the process of case advocacy?

The power of a case manager lies in his or her capacity to organize and manipulate the human service environment so that it becomes more responsive to the client (Albert, 1985). Case managers regularly overlook several sources of power available to them. These include:

1. Authority.   Case managers may work for agencies which have the formal authority (i.e., the formal right) to enforce access to services and

the adherence to standards of care. This authority may evolve out of the legislative, legal, or administrative mandate of the case management agency.

2. Human Resources.   The case manager can access people who will cooperate with him or her in redressing a denial of services or benefits. Such human resources include other professionals, organized consumer groups, and watchdog organizations such as rights protection and advocacy agencies.

3. Skill and knowledge.   The case manager may have detailed knowledge of eligibility, licensing, and standards guiding services. This knowledge and related skills can be used to demand services from a particular agency.

4. Social psychological factors.   The case manager may be charismatic, influential, or have an exemplary reputation within the community, all of which can contribute to an agency's willingness to respect and respond to his or her wishes.

5. Material Resources.   The case manager may be able to access funds in order to purchase services from providers. The case manager can use these funds to motivate an agency to serve a particular client either by purchasing service or by withdrawing funds if the agency is not responsive.

What tactics can case managers use to influence human services agencies? The following are examples of several types of tactics the case manager can employ in case advocacy. These vary along a continuum that ranges from influence strategies such as bargaining to conflict-laden strategies involving confrontation.

1. Negotiate and bargain with frontline and middle level personnel.

2. Direct appeals through the organizational network following chain of command. Emphasize mission of the agency, the goals of the agency, and its philosophy if these are relevant.

3. Invoke the legal mandate of the agency especially if the agency is neglecting to serve a person who has been identified as within the scope of agency services.

4. Appeal to an external ombudsman to intervene and reconcile the problem of access.

5. Go to the funding sources of the agency and make argument that the organization is not being accountable in the use of its services, funds, and resources.

6. Seek media exposure and make an issue of the agency not serving a particular client or group of clients.

7. Collaborate with organized consumer groups in confronting the agency.

8. Use institutional systems of rights protection and advocacy, legal rights, or pro bono legal assistance agencies in seeking redress, possibly through the courts.

The strategy of the case manager is to resolve the problem at the lowest level of conflict possible. Before escalating the conflict the case manager must be certain that all avenues of influence, negotiation, and bargaining have been employed. The case manager also must be aware of the personal cost that may be involved in case advocacy. The process calls for the case manager to accept vulnerability and possible retaliation while attempting to redress any wrongs done to a client.

Advocacy activities are summarized in Table 5.4.

BUILDING RESPONSIVE SOCIAL NETWORKS

The mutual care component of the client service network can provide a significant source of support for the clients of case managers. The social network composed of family, friends, informal helpers, and others can provide resources to clients that may not be available or attainable through formal human service delivery systems. Through natural networks of social support clients can gain:

1. Emotional support and tangible assistance relating to specific problems of community or daily living.
2. A reference group of individuals who experience a problem similar to the clients and who can provide insight and knowledge regarding how to cope effectively with such a problem (Hepworth & Larsen, 1982).
3. Hope and inspiration about overcoming one's problem in the future.

There are a number of activities that case managers can undertake in their work with the mutual care component of the client support network. Three categories of case management intervention activities are significant here. These are (1) educational activities undertaken with members of the social network, (2) second order support activities, and (3) alternative support systems. Each of these is briefly discussed.

1. Educational Activities

The goal of these intervention activities is to increase the understanding of social network members of the needs of the client, and of the ways members can respond to these needs. A basic intervention activity may involve educating family members, friends, and others about the disabilities or problems of the client. Such educational activities can be tailored to individual social networks; or, alternatively, these networks can be combined and offered large group educational programs. An example of the former

TABLE 5.4   An Overview of Case Advocacy

GOAL OF STRATEGY

To confront agency that refuses to serve client and motivate it to serve client

ELEMENTS OF STRATEGY

1. Powerbase of case manager:
    —Authority
    —Human resources
    —Skill and knowledge
    —Social psychological factors
    —Material resources
2. Implement tactics but attempt to resolve issue at the lowest level of conflict:
    —Negotiate and bargain with organizational actors
    —Direct appeals through organizational network
    —Invoke legal mandate of agency
    —Appeal to external ombudsman
    —Go to funding sources
    —Seek media exposure
    —Mobilize organized consumer groups
    —Use institutional systems of rights protection and advocacy

---

is the case manager conducting several educational sessions for an extended family of a young adult who is coping with schizophrenia. The family can be oriented to the nature of schizophrenia, problems the young adult may encounter, and effective ways to cope with this disorder (Falloon, Boyd, & McGill, 1984).

On the other hand, the case manager may organize an educational program on severe mental illness for several families with the goal not only of providing family education, but also developing external sources of support that go beyond the immediate family. Through this activity the case manager also engages in the development of self-help groups or "alternative sources of support."

In addition, the educational and training content of sessions can be expanded to include instruction in giving support, in assuming and managing caregiving roles, and in coping effectively with the stress that can arise from living with and supporting a person with problems of social functioning (Springer & Brubaker, 1984).

2. Second Order Support Activities

When involving social network members in the care and support of clients it is imperative that the case manager assess the capacities of network members to carry through with these responsibilities. If the assessment identifies problems with coping, stress, and resources, the case manager should build into the intervention process plans for the organization, delivery, and maintenance of "second order" supports.

These supports involve the provision of social and tangible assistance to individuals providing first-order support to the client. For example, family members who are caring for an adolescent who has a severe developmental disability may need access to respite care, to transportation, and to periodic homemaker services.

The burnout of primary care providers is a problem inherent in the development of the mutual care component of the client support network. The case manager can plan and respond to the contingencies of stress and burnout by:

(1) Working with primary caregivers to identify roles and functions that they can successfully execute within their available resources.

(2) Augmenting the resources of the social network as a means of buffering the experience of stress and strain. These can include the use of case aides to transport clients to appointments, the use of homemaker services, in-home respite services so that significant others can take care of other responsibilities, and the use of home visits.

(3) Arranging or providing access to crisis intervention, counseling, or psycho-therapeutic services if these are desired by social network members.

3. Alternative Support System Activities

These activities are related to both educational activities and second-order support activities. The case manager identifies opportunities for social network members to participate in self-help groups, consumer groups, or other organized sources of support. As noted above, these alternative support systems can provide social network members with opportunities to interact with family members or relatives of other clients who are experiencing the same type of problem.

The case manager can identify alternative support systems while developing the resource inventory during the process of client needs assessment. Alternatively, the case manager can refer social network members to information and referral services designed to link family members to social support, educational, or self-help resources.

In some cases the case manager may collaborate with social network members in creating alternative support systems. The indigenous leadership, skills, and energy of social network members can be integrated with the case manager's knowledge of resources and organizational skills to create new sources of support for family members and significant others (Baker, 1977; Gottlieb & Schroter, 1978; Lenrow & Burch, 1981).

Table 5.5 provides an overview of activities relevant to the development and support of social networks.

PROVIDING TECHNICAL ASSISTANCE AND CONSULTATION

The final indirect service function examined here is that of technical assistance and consultation. Case managers, in fulfilling their systemic roles within human service delivery systems, have opportunities to work with large groups of clients, with diverse human service organizations and resource systems, with informal support systems, and with other community systems. They are therefore likely to develop considerable expertise in responding to specific client problems, and an extensive knowledge of the strengths and limitations of service delivery networks.

The case manager can make a contribution to strengthening the responsiveness of agencies to client needs by fulfilling technical assistance and consultation roles. These terms mean that case managers can serve change agentry functions by introducing new knowledge, information, and perspectives into human service agencies as a means of improving service delivery to selected clients or groups of clients (Gallessich, 1982).

For example, the case manager may be sensitive to the need for new programs to serve homebound elderly persons. The needs of this population and ways to serve these clients can be imparted by the case manager to an agency with the goal of encouraging the development of a new program. In this example the case manager is enabling an agency to stay current with client needs and facilitating change in the community service delivery network (O'Neill & Trickett, 1982; Parsons & Meyers, 1984).

The aim of technical assistance and consultation on the part of the case manager is utilitarian. The case manager is interested in new approaches to client service delivery. He or she is therefore willing to impart information, equip the consultee with relevant knowledge, and provide support for the consultee to try new approaches.

To execute this strategy the case manager relies on education and the exchange of knowledge. As noted above, the basis of the case manager's expertise is both professional and experiential. The latter evolves out of the case manager's understanding of the "big picture," of the strengths and limitations of the service delivery network, of gaps in the service delivery network, and of unmet client needs. This knowledge is obtained largely from the information the case manager derives from the manage-

TABLE 5.5   An Overview of Building Social Networks

GOAL OF STRATEGY
Develop mutual care component of client support network

ELEMENTS OF STRATEGY
1. Benefits derived from social networks:
   —Emotional support
   —Tangible assistance
   —Reference group
   —Hope and inspiration
2. Case management intervention activities with social network members:
   —Education of network members
   —Second order support of network members
   —Alternative support systems

---

ment of his or her caseload, which involves interaction with a number of human service agencies.

Technical assistance and consultation involves a prescribed sequence of activities. These include:

1. Responding to an agency's request for assistance and consultation in relationship to a specific client problem or service delivery problem. Alternatively, the case manager, recognizing unmet client needs, may contact agency representatives to apprise them of this situation.

2. Educating the agency about the parameters of the unmet needs especially as they relate to demographic, socioeconomic, or diagnostic factors. The case manager imparts information derived from his or her caseload or from the unmet needs reflected in the clients who are referred to the agency.

3. Exploration of the approaches that can be used to remedy the service delivery problem or to fulfill unmet needs. The case manager may consult with the agency in identifying prescriptive actions or may participate in an agency task force which will attempt to identify a programmatic response.

4. Provide support to the agency in its efforts to develop a programmatic response to the identified problem or need. Such support may involve the case manager in writing letters of support, participating in resource development, or in providing testimony to appropriate funding sources.

The long range implication of this indirect service strategy is a systemic one (O'Neill & Trickett, 1982). That is, through technical assistance and consultation the case manager seeks to change the service delivery system by encouraging the development of new services and programs designed to fulfill unmet client needs.

Table 5.6 summarizes the technical assistance and consultation strategy.

CONCLUSION

The indirect service function involves the case manager in using different strategies to develop a responsive client support network. In some cases, as with brokering and linkage, the indirect service function serves to connect clients with existing services, and to assure that these services are both used and delivered in the appropriate manner. Alternatively, as with advocacy strategy, the case manager may use influence or even conflict techniques as a means of obtaining responsiveness from service providers.

Other strategies composing the indirect service function are based more on developing and maintaining cooperation among service providers and social network members. Thus, the coordination strategy recognizes the difficulty involved in getting human service providers to cooperate with one another. Yet, case managers must use tactics that increase the probability of client-level coordination. When working with social networks, the case manager must assure that members of these networks have the knowledge, skills, and supports they need to serve as effective providers of informal care and social support.

Finally, the systemic nature of case management is reflected in technical assistance and consultation strategies. It is these strategies that focus the case manager's efforts on the translation of systemic knowledge of unmet needs and gaps in service delivery into action to resolve these problems at the level of an agency or a service delivery system.

At the core of the indirect service function must be the recognition that the case manager often serves as the "hub" of a complex interagency network. Probably the most powerful strategy case managers can employ is to use this network in responding to the needs of their clients.

EXERCISES

1. Select a current case. For this case indicate how you can use the six indirect service strategies to improve the delivery of services to this client.

TABLE 5.6   An Overview of Technical Assistance and Consultation

---

GOAL OF STRATEGY
Promote change and innovation of human services in meeting client needs

ELEMENTS OF STRATEGY
1. Case manager's knowledge and expertise:
   —Professional skills and competencies
   —Experiential knowledge
   —Awareness of client needs, service delivery problems
2. Steps in provision of technical assistance and consultation:
   —Responding to agency's request for assistance
   —Approaching agency representatives to apprise them of client needs
   —Educating agency about unmet needs and relevant characteristics of clients
   —Exploring approaches to resolving service delivery problems
   —Participating in design of programmatic response
   —Supporting agency in obtaining resources to implement programmatic response

---

2. Using the indirect service function of coordination, outline ways in which you can improve the cooperation of agencies in providing services to the client you selected above.

3. For the clients you have served in the past month, to what extent have you engaged in case advocacy? What tactics have you used in operationalizing case advocacy?

4. Review your current caseload with the purpose of identifying (1) unmet client needs, (2) gaps in agency services, and (3) ideas for new programs or services. Review this profile, and identify a systemic agenda for improving the service delivery network within your community.

Chapter 6

The Monitoring Function of Case Management

KEY QUESTIONS

---

1. What is the role of service and support monitoring in case management practice?

2. What are four dimensions of service and support monitoring?

3. How does the case manager make use of an informal and qualitative approach to service and support monitoring?

4. How does the case manager make use of a formal and quantitative approach to service and support monitoring?

5. What are some of the major tools used by the case manager in service and support monitoring?

INTRODUCTION AND GOALS OF CHAPTER

This chapter presents an approach to monitoring client services and supports as a means of maintaining the momentum of service delivery. Case managers work under different constraints and mandates. For monitoring to be a successful function these limitations and circumstances must be recognized. Thus, the purpose of this chapter is to outline a framework of monitoring that is relevant to the varying circumstances of case management practice. The goals of this chapter are to:

1. Identify the role of monitoring in the practice of case management.
2. Identify relevant dimensions of monitoring.
3. Explain two types of monitoring that can be used by case managers depending on their practice situations.
4. Present a framework of the monitoring function, and discuss the process of monitoring incorporated within this framework.

DEFINITION AND PURPOSE OF SERVICE AND SUPPORT MONITORING

Service and support monitoring is identified as an important function in many models of case management. Monitoring connotes an active and fluid process (Morris & Fitz-Gibbon, 1978b; Patton, 1987) implemented by the case manager as a means of tracking the delivery of services and supports which have been identified within the client's master plan. The case manager uses this process to determine how well the service plan is being implemented by members of the client support network. Monitoring, therefore, involves the collection, review, analysis, and interpretation of service and support data (Epstein & Tripodi, 1977; King, Morris, & Fitz-Gibbon, 1987; Thomas, 1984). Monitoring is then executed by the case manager during the actual process of service delivery.

Essentially the case manager uses the monitoring function as a tool in following the progress of the implementation of the service plan. Consistent with the model of case management outlined in Chapter 1, the focus of the case manager is the development of a client support network while the mission of the case manager is to sustain this network over time. Monitoring plays a key role in the case manager's effort to sustain the client support network.

Monitoring serves four purposes in the practice of case management. Basically these purposes are to:

1. Determine the extent to which the service plan is being implemented appropriately.   Chapter 3 identifies the critical attributes of the client service and support plan. One attribute most salient in relationship to monitoring is the role of the plan as a guidance system. The plan guides the case manager in monitoring the tasks, activities, and responsibilities of those individuals

involved in providing services and supports. Monitoring is used by the case manager to assure that members of the client support network are implementing the substance and specifications of the plan.

2. Determine the achievement of the objectives of the client service and support plan.   The objectives of the client service and support plan are designed to identify what will be delivered or provided in order to address the fulfillment of the client's needs. Monitoring is a tool the case manager uses to follow the accomplishment of the objectives of the plan. Through consistent monitoring the case manager can determine whether objectives are being achieved, whether they are being achieved according to the timeline, or whether there is failure to achieve objectives.

In fulfilling this function the case manager uses monitoring as an accountability mechanism (King, Morris, & Fitz-Gibbon, 1987). Exercising consistent oversight means that the case manager assumes accountability for assuring appropriate implementation of the client service and support plan. Alternatively, the case manager uses monitoring as an accountability mechanism by ''flagging'' unfulfilled objectives, and by following up with those individuals responsible for activities that will lead to the accomplishment of service and support objectives.

3. Determine service and support outcomes.   The service delivery process is a dynamic one characterized by, under ideal circumstances, progressive movement toward the fulfillment of client needs. However, implementation of the client service and support plan may not lead to need fulfillment. So, monitoring allows the case manager to track outcomes over time. If the implementation of the plan is not leading to client need fulfillment, monitoring serves as a trigger for convening a meeting to revise the client service and support plan.

4. Identify the emergence of new client needs requiring change in the service plan.   Over time new client needs will emerge as the lives, environments, or circumstances of clients change. Monitoring enables the case manager to track emerging needs and to communicate these needs to the client support network. By monitoring the emergence of new needs the case manager assures that the plan and resulting service provision are both relevant.

DIMENSIONS OF MONITORING

With these purposes of monitoring in mind, we can identify several dimensions of this function. The case manager can employ these dimensions in focusing his or her monitoring tasks. They involve (1) effort, (2) adequacy, (3) quality, and (4) outcome.

1. Effort. The case manager is concerned with the extent to which members of the client support network are accomplishing objectives, fulfilling specified activities, executing their responsibilities, and following timelines.

2. Adequacy. The case manager is concerned with whether the client plan has the necessary services and supports to address the client's needs at a given time. This is especially important in obtaining information necessary to the adaptation of the plan to changes in client environment or needs.

3. Quality. The case manager is concerned with how well the client service and support plan is being implemented.

4. Outcome. The case manager is concerned with the extent to which the plan either succeeds, or creates adverse outcomes.

TYPES OF MONITORING

The case manger has a choice in structuring the monitoring function. Considerations such as time, technology, size of caseload, and breadth of responsibilities must be taken into consideration when choosing the form, tools, and techniques of monitoring. There are two major approaches to monitoring: (1) informal and qualitative; and (2) formal and quantitative (Thomas, 1984).

INFORMAL AND QUALITATIVE

This type of monitoring is impressionistic, free-flowing, and implemented by the case manager on an informal basis. The case manager employing this type of monitoring uses himself or herself as the monitoring instrument. He or she relies on judgment in determining whether the client service and support plan is being implemented appropriately and leading to desired outcomes.

Case managers may choose this type of monitoring when they experience time and resource constraints, or when they do not want to appear intrusive. Rather than failing to monitor, the case manager makes it a more feasible but a less rigorous process than formal/quantitative monitoring.

A number of monitoring techniques are relevant here. These include correspondence with clients, social network members, or service providers, informal meetings with members of the client support network, telephone contacts, review of case records, and crisis contacts with the client.

FORMAL AND QUANTITATIVE

This type of monitoring is structured, proceduralized, and formalized. It is implemented by the case manager using either the standards of the monitoring instruments and/or the monitoring standards of the case management program. Rather than relying on judgment exclusively, the case manager may employ normative and criterion-oriented standards in monitoring effort, adequacy, quality, and outcome.

The choice of this type of monitoring may be specified more by the purpose and mandate of the case management program than by the conditions under which the case manager is working. For example, state mandate may require a case management program to monitor the functional status of clients with developmental disabilities using a standardized instrument. The program may be accountable for reporting to another organization standardized data about individual and aggregate client progress.

Tools that can be used by the case manager are quite varied. They can include structured questionnaires or interview instruments formulated by case managers themselves, structured checklists for auditing client records, and standardized functional scales used to assess the development and behavior of clients.

Case managers may incorporate monitoring tools into the assessment process. This allows them not only to capture relevant assessment data, but to obtain a baseline on the functional status or behavior of the client. These tools can then be used for the purposes of monitoring at selected points of the intervention process. Monitoring indicators can then be compared to indicators of client status at time of initial assessment to determine whether there was any change.

A MODEL OF
THE CASE MANAGEMENT MONITORING FUNCTION

Table 6.1 presents a model of the case management monitoring function. This model can be employed by case managers in planning their monitoring strategy. It is consistent with the overall framework of case management presented in this book. Chapter 1 discussed the focus of case management as being the development and maintenance of a client support net-

TABLE 6.1   A Model of the Case Management Monitoring Function

		Types of Monitoring	
		Type I Effort Adequacy Quality Outcome	Type II Effort Adequacy Quality Outcome
Dimensions of Client Support Network	*Client Self-Care*		
	Mutual Care	Type III Effort Adequacy Quality Outcome	Type IV Effort Adequacy Quality Outcome
	Professional Care	Type V Effort Adequacy Quality Outcome	Type VI Effort Adequacy Quality Outcome

work. Thus, the client support network should also be the focus of the case manager's monitoring function.

As noted above the case manager also may choose to engage in either informal/qualitative monitoring or, alternatively, formal/quantitative monitoring. However, whichever type the case manager chooses he or she can address four dimensions of monitoring: effort, adequacy, quality, and outcome.

Finally, the case manager's monitoring activities are directed by the client service and support plan. This plan, as identified in Chapter 3, identifies service and support objectives, as well as the roles of the client, social network members, and other professionals in achieving these objectives.

Table 6.1 summarizes these different aspects of monitoring and identifies six varieties of the monitoring function. Let us briefly review each one:

1. Informal/qualitative monitoring of client self-care (Type I).   This approach to monitoring focuses the case manager's attention on the extent to which clients are using their own skills, abilities, and capacities in fulfilling their needs. Key questions for the case manager include whether the client is making an effort, consistent with the service and support plan, to implement activities necessary to the achievement of objectives, whether the identified self-care activities are adequate to the fulfillment of the plan, whether these activities are being undertaken appropriately, and whether these ac-

tivities are leading to the fulfillment of client needs. Tools the case manager can employ in this form of monitoring include informal observation of the client, home visits, face-to-face meetings, and telephone contacts.

2. Formal/quantitative monitoring of client self-care (Type II). This form of monitoring requires the case manager to use a systematic approach. The monitoring questions identified in Type I monitoring are still relevant. Yet, the case manager uses structured approaches to the collection and interpretation of data. For example, the case manager may employ a "self-care rating scale" that provides the case manager and client feedback regarding whether the client is engaging in activities of daily living (i.e., the effort dimension), and how well the client is executing these tasks (i.e., the quality dimension).

3. Informal/qualitative monitoring of mutual care (Type III). In this form of monitoring the case manager focuses on the extent to which social network members are contributing to the achievement of client service and support objectives. The case manager is concerned with the effort of these network members and whether the activities they are undertaking are adequate to the fulfillment of the identified objectives. In addition, the case manager monitors the quality of support activities and the contribution of these activities to the fulfillment of client needs. Techniques that the case manager uses here can include informal meetings of network members, unstructured questionnaires requesting input from network members, telephone contacts, and critical incidents that occur during a crisis episode.

4. Formal/quantitative monitoring of mutual care (Type IV). This type of monitoring involves the case manager in the systematic collection of data regarding the provision of social supports to the client. The case manager may ask social network members to maintain logs or diaries summarizing their social support efforts and activities. Other tools include the use of rating tools that give a profile of the frequency of social support activities, and structured feedback questionnaires through which social network members can identify their concerns or problems with the roles they have assumed.

5. Informal/qualitative monitoring of professional care (Type V). This type of monitoring focuses the case manager's attention on the activities of other professionals providing services to the client. Again, the core monitoring dimensions are effort (whether the professionals are following through with prescribed activities), adequacy (whether these activities or services are necessary to the fulfillment of client needs), quality (how well these professionals are delivering services), and outcome (whether these services are contributing to the fulfillment of client needs). The case manager uses tools such as informal meetings or contacts, site visits, telephone con-

tacts, and the unstructured review of client records to obtain information necessary for monitoring the delivery of professional services.

6. Formal/quantitative monitoring of professional care (Type VI). The case manager uses this type of monitoring when there is a need for formal accountability measures guiding service delivery to the client by other professionals. The case manager addresses effort, adequacy, quality, and outcome through the use of (1) official milestone meetings during which services are reviewed and evaluated, (2) systematic audit of records focusing on the identification of types of services, length of interaction, the adequacy of clinical notation, as well as the identification of client progress and benefits, and (3) structured instruments which require service providers to self-evaluate their contributions to client care and support.

Successful monitoring does not necessarily require the case manager to use formal and quantitative approaches exclusively. My recommendation is that the case manager prioritize "comprehensive monitoring" in which he or she attempts to monitor all the major components of the client support network. The case manager can then combine both formal and informal techniques to achieve this goal. A combination of techniques will enable the case manager to increase the probability of identifying areas of self-care, social support, and professional care in which there are problems, weaknesses, or concerns among the people who are serving in various service and support roles. This strategy may also enable the case manager to create an approach to monitoring that is compatible with workload and other professional responsibilities.

A NOTE ON THE PROCESS OF MONITORING

Like the other case management functions, monitoring is a continuous process of determining whether the objectives of the client service and support plan are being fulfilled, and whether the activities, responsibilities and timelines essential to the achievement of objectives are being executed by those individuals identified within the plan.

The monitoring process as an ongoing professional activity requires the case manager to plan continually for this activity. A relatively simple process can be implemented by the case manager to assure that he or she executes this function on a regular basis. This process involves the following steps:

1. The case manager assesses his or her own time constraints, professional responsibilities, and organizational context. Based on this self-assessment he or she then selects an appropriate type or mix of monitoring approaches (i. e. formal, informal, or a mix of the two).

2. The case manager identifies the major tasks and activities relating to the monitoring of client self-care, mutual care, and professional care, and the types of monitoring selected.

3. For each component of the client support network the case manager identifies a monitoring objective that focuses on effort, adequacy, quality, or outcome. Ideally the case manager will attempt to address all of these dimensions, but this may not be feasible.

4. For each monitoring objective the case manager identifies:
   a. The people who will participate in monitoring.
   b. The tools or approaches the case manager will use to collect data.
   c. The timeline for conducting monitoring activities.
   d. Action steps the case manager will take based on the data (i.e., to change some aspect of the client service and support plan, or to convene a team to review client services and supports).

CONCLUSION

Monitoring is means of following the implementation of service delivery and the provision of social support to a client. This function is designed to serve as a "self-correction" mechanism. As noted at the beginning of this chapter, monitoring enables the case manager to "stay on top of" implementation and to determine achievement of objectives, the appropriateness of implementation, whether services and supports are making a difference in the life of the client, and whether there is a need for changing the service and support plan. So, in a sense, the monitoring function serves as a "self-correction" mechanism whereby the case manager, on a frequent or periodic basis, reviews the implementation of the service and support plan to determine whether aspects of this plan must be modified in order to address client needs better. Through consistent monitoring the case manager is able to serve in a "formative" role in which she or he uses data to improve the delivery of services and supports while the plan is being implemented.

EXERCISES

1. Take time to reflect on your current position and assess the size of your caseload, the range of your professional responsibilities, and the other factors influenc-

ing your position. Based on your assessment, what approach to monitoring appears to be feasible for you? A formal one? An informal one? Write down a rationale for your decision.

2. Select a client record. Review this record and attempt to identify the monitoring activities you have undertaken or ones which have been undertaken by others. Reflect on the strengths and weaknesses of these monitoring activities.

3. Select a client for whom you have not been monitoring service delivery. Construct a monitoring plan for this client using the steps outlined in this chapter.

Chapter 7

The Evaluation Function of Case Management

KEY QUESTIONS

---

1. How can we define evaluation in the context of case management practice?

2. What is the role of the evaluation function in case management practice?

3. What are four key evaluation questions and related approaches to evaluation?

4. What are the major steps involved in formulating a plan for evaluating the attainment of impact goals?

5. What is the difference between a social role approach to the evaluation of functioning versus a task-focused approach?

6. Why is the client service and support plan an object of evaluation?

7. Why is the evaluation of client satisfaction a relevant means of determining the worth of case management?

INTRODUCTION

At the root of the term "evaluation" is the concept of value. This concept is important in considering the evaluation function of case management since "value" gets to the heart of understanding the purpose and nature of evaluation. According to Stufflebeam and Shinkfield (1986), evaluation involves the "determination of the worth of an object." Thus, in the context of case management, evaluation is a process employed to determine whether the service plan, service components, and service activities mobilized and coordinated by the case manager are worthwhile. Ultimately, the case manager must be concerned about whether the client is realizing beneficial outcomes as a result of participating in the case management process. Evaluation is a function employed by the case manager to attain this end.

The evaluation function employed by case managers is different from the monitoring function discussed in the previous chapter. Whereas monitoring addresses the primary question of whether identified activities are being implemented in a planned way, evaluation focuses on whether these activities are producing beneficial and desirable outcomes. Use of the monitoring function directs the attention of the case manager to the consideration of whether the goals and objectives identified in the client service plan are being realized as a means of forming and sustaining the client support network over time.

Yet the focus of monitoring, for the most part, is on implementation. Although there is some overlap between evaluation and monitoring, the former is concerned with ascertaining whether case management activities are making a difference in the life of the client.

By employing the evaluation function, case managers can express their concern for determining the beneficial aspects of client outcome in several different ways. One way is by questioning whether the client service and support plan is a worthwhile one. By responding to this evaluation question the case manager deals with the issue of whether the plan should be modified or whether a whole new plan must be developed. A second way is by examining specific impact goals: Is the achievement of impact goals making a positive (or perhaps a negative) difference in the need areas specified by these goals?

Closely related here is a third focus of evaluation. Overall, is the implementation of the client service and support plan making a difference in the life of the client? Here case managers use the evaluation function to address "bottom-line" issues: does implementation of the client service and support plan increase the functioning of the client? Or, does the implementation of the plan enhance the quality of life of the client? A final way of examining outcomes of the case management process is by evaluating the extent to which a client (or a client advocate) is satisfied with the service and support plan, the implementation of the service and support plan, and the effectiveness of the service and supports delivered to the client (Berger, 1983).

These four ways of examining the worth of case management services provide case managers with several different options for implementing the evaluation function. These four approaches enable case managers to expand the means by which they determine the worth of the case management process by addressing (1) relevance of the service and support plan, (2) goal attainment and impact, (3) general effectiveness, and (4) client satisfaction.

GOALS OF THE CHAPTER

The purpose of this chapter is to discuss these different approaches to the case management evaluation function. More specifically, the goals of this chapter are to:

1. Identify the role of evaluation in the practice of case management.
2. Elaborate on four approaches to the evaluation of the worth of the services and supports developed and implemented by the case manager.
3. Discuss the major steps in implementing each of the major approaches to case management evaluation.

FOUR APPROACHES TO CASE MANAGEMENT EVALUATION

EVALUATION OF THE CLIENT SERVICE AND SUPPORT PLAN

When engaging in this form of evaluation the case manager is concerned with determining the worth of the client service and support plan. This plan, as emphasized in Chapter 3, guides the provision of the services and supports to the client, and reflects the formulation of the client support network. Monitoring is used by the case manager to track whether this plan is being implemented in the appropriate manner.

Yet, it is critical for the case manager to question the overall contribution of the service and support plan to the well-being of the client. Evaluation is important, therefore, as the means by which this determination is undertaken by the case manager. There are several reasons why this determination is important.

First, the client service and support plan is indeed a "plan." Case managers, the client, members of the client's social network, and other professionals composing the interdisciplinary team have no absolute assurance that this plan will work. The plan is rather a projection of what "should be done" and is based on the best judgment of the individuals making up the planning team. Given the tentative nature of the plan, the case manager is advised to remain somewhat skeptical of its general appropriateness and effectiveness, and to use evaluation as a means of determining its worth at later stages of service provision, when the plan is actually being implemented.

Second, there is a quality assurance dimension to the evaluation of the client service and support plan. The case manager wants to make certain that the resources the plan requires for effective implementation are adequate. Thus, the overall evaluation of the plan's worth must include a determination of whether inputs are adequate to meet the identified needs of the client.

There is another aspect to this quality assurance dimension which we can label "process." It is here that evaluation is closely aligned with monitoring. When evaluating the worth of the client service and support plan the case manager is concerned with determining whether the plan is being implemented in an appropriate and beneficial manner. The case manager should not expect the plan to create beneficial outcomes if the activities and tasks composing the plan are being implemented incorrectly.

A third reason for the client service and support plan acting as a target of evaluation lies in utilization review. The key evaluation question here is "whether the plan remains relevant as a tool for meeting the needs of the client?" During the process of service delivery the client's needs may have changed dramatically. Of course, ongoing implementation by the case manager of the functions of assessment and monitoring may identify the need to modify the client service and support plan. However, it is possible that the client has reached a point when an entirely new plan should be developed, or when the client should terminate case management services.

Utilization review is an important evaluative concept because it raises the question "what does the client still need?" Here the case manager faces the problem of context evaluation (Stufflebeam & Shinkfield, 1986); that is, whether the plan as formulated meets the emergent needs of the client.

The client service and support plan, as an object of evaluation, therefore, involves three foci which are listed below:

1. The evaluation of inputs.   Of importance here is evaluating whether the people, services, and other resources composing the plan are adequate to attain the impact goals delineated within the plan.

2. The evaluation of process.   Here the case manager is concerned with

TABLE 7.1   Unstructured Questionnaire for Obtaining Feedback
about the Client Service and Support Plan

As a member of the team which has been involved in planning and providing services to Joe Meyers, the XYZ case management agency is asking you to participate in a meeting during which we will evaluate the services Mr. Meyers has been receiving. In preparation for this meeting, we ask you to take a moment to respond to the questions listed below and to return these to our agency before August 10, 1988. Thank you for your involvement, and we look forward to seeing you at the meeting on September 20, 1988.

1. Overall, is the case management plan still relevant to the needs of Mr. Meyers?

2. Do the goals remain relevant to meeting the needs of Mr. Meyers?

3. Has Mr. Meyers developed new needs which suggest to you that the current plan needs to be revised? How should we revise the current plan in light of these new needs?

4. Are the services identified in the plan still relevant to meeting the needs of Mr. Meyers?

5. From your perspective, are the services identified in the current plan being provided to Mr. Meyers in a timely and an appropriate manner?

6. Are the activities and tasks of specific people identified in the plan being completed in a timely and an appropriate manner?

_____

_____

_____

7. Do you have any other comments you want to share with us about Mr. Meyers' service and support plan?

_____

_____

_____

whether the activities and tasks delineated within the client service and support plan are being undertaken in the appropriate manner.

3. The evaluation of context.   Here the case manager is concerned with whether the client service and support plan is designed to meet the needs of the client, especially those needs which have emerged through ongoing assessment and monitoring of the client support network.

How does the case manager conduct an evaluation of the client service and support plan? A number of methods are available ranging from highly structured to unstructured. A major tool for this approach to evaluation, however, is the use of the interdisciplinary team as a means of collecting observations of the worth of the client service and support plan. This assumes that the case manager includes in the membership of this team the client, his or her representatives, and members of the client's social network.

The case manager convenes the team with the specific purpose of evaluating the plan. Structured evaluative information can be collected from team members beforehand through the use of a checklist or a questionnaire. An example of a questionnaire useful in obtaining feedback regarding inputs, process, and context of the plan is displayed in Table 7.1. One advantage to using either structured or unstructured questionnaires is that they enable the case manager to obtain and organize information before the evaluation meeting. Also, the case manager is able to aggregate the data regarding the plan in order to assemble information about the general perceptions of team members. However, unlike the structured questionnaire, the unstructured alternative may require the case manager to invest more time in assembling and summarizing information.

The case manager can employ structured and/or unstructured techniques in conducting the evaluative meeting. Unstructured techniques involve such activities as open discussion, brainstorming, and spontaneous comments. Although such techniques may be a good means of generating evaluative statements about the plan, they may suppress contributions from less assertive members.

Structured meeting techniques such as nominal group process (Delbecq, Van de Ven, & Gustafson, 1975; Moore, 1987) are one means of involving less assertive members and counteracting "group think." Yet structured techniques may require much time, and restrain the generation of novel observations.

Meetings called by the case manager to evaluate the client service and support plan can combine both structured and unstructured procedures. These procedures will help expedite the meeting, involve all team members, and encourage the identification of what is working and what is not working. The procedures outlined in Table 7.2 may prove useful in conducting an evaluation of the client service and support plan.

The team convened to conduct the evaluation of the client service and support plan is not necessarily a decision-making group. The case manager and the client must ultimately control the client service and support plan. In addition, as discussed below in the section on client satisfaction, feedback from the client regarding the plan is most important. Yet the evaluative meeting serves as a mechanism for bringing together all of the major actors involved in implementing the plan. It therefore expands the range of information available to the case manager and to the client. This information may assist the case manager and the client in identifying and considering more options than if they limited the evaluation of the service and support plan to themselves.

EVALUATION OF THE ATTAINMENT OF IMPACT GOALS

The evaluation of goal attainment actually begins the case manager's consideration of the outcomes produced by the case management process (Morris & Fitz-Gibbon, 1978c). As emphasized in Chapter 3, the client service and support plan is composed, in part, of impact goals that are tied to the identified needs of the client. Take, for example, the social contact goals which were designed to address Mrs. Williams's social and interpersonal needs:

TABLE 7.2 Suggested Procedures for Conducting an Evaluation Meeting

1. Disseminate data gathering instruments prior to the meeting so that team members have an opportunity to think about the client service and support plan and to evaluate the plan.
2. Summarize responses to the evaluative questions prior to the meeting either by calculating simple descriptive statistics in the case of structured questionnaires or by categorizing similar observations in the case of unstructured questionnaires.
3. If possible, prior to the evaluation meeting, disseminate the summarized data with a written notation of the general strengths and weaknesses of the plan.
4. Begin the meeting with an overview of the evaluative data collected through the questionnaires and a summary of the strengths and weaknesses of the plan. Open the meeting to a general discussion of the information and the strengths and limitations of the plan as reflected by the questionnaires.
5. Provide members with a five to ten minute period during which they can identify one or two additional observations about the strengths and limitations of the client service and support plan.
6. Open the meeting to a brief discussion of these new observations during which they are listed on a blackboard or on newsprint.
7. Ask members to identify on their own several issues relating to the client service and support plan that should be revised, eliminated, strengthened.
8. Ask members to prioritize (perhaps through a vote) those issues that are most important to change in the client service and support plan.
9. The identified issues and their prioritization can then be used by the client and the case manager as issues to consider in the revision of the client service and support plan.

1. To increase the frequency of social contact between Mrs. Williams and her neighbors.
2. To increase the frequency of social contact between Mrs. Williams and her grandchildren.
3. To increase the frequency of social contact between Mrs. Williams and peers of her own age.

These goals were formulated as a means of increasing the social support available to Mrs. Williams which, in turn, was tied to the problem of sustaining her independent living. The problem for the case manager is twofold here and illustrates the importance of evaluating whether the attainment of these goals fulfills the client's ultimate need.

One aspect of this problem is whether goals have actually been fulfilled. In the case of Mrs. Williams, the case manager is interested in whether the level of social contact Mrs. Williams has with neighbors, grandchildren, and peers has actually increased. A second aspect of this problem is whether the increase of social contact is enabling Mrs. Williams to live safely and independently in her own home.

Let us deal with the issue of ascertaining the achievement of the specific outcome delineated by the impact goal. The example of Mrs. Williams will help us here. In her case, the goal of increasing social contact with neighbors, grandchildren, and peers has been delineated as an important outcome. Thus, the case manager is attempting to expand her social network by increasing the actors composing this network and by increasing the frequency of interaction with significant others.

A formal evaluation of the attainment of this goal involves the case manager in several design decisions, the culmination of which forms the plan for the evaluation of the attainment of impact goals. These decisions include the following:

1. Stating the impact goal. The statement of the impact goal is taken directly from the client service and support plan.

2. Identifying the key concepts for measurement. The case manager identifies the key concepts for measurement. In the social and interpersonal need areas for Mrs. Williams there is one key concept. This is the concept of social contact. The case manager will want to be very specific here because social contact could include mail, telephone, or face-to-face contact. In this situation we are concerned with the last of these.

3. Delineation of indicators. What factors are indicative of the concept which the case manager is attempting to evaluate? Such indicators may be behavioral, attitudinal, perceptual, or physical. In Mrs. Williams's situation the case manager is concerned with two indicators: 1) increased frequency of contact between the client and others; and 2) increased frequency of contact with specific types of people (neighbors, grandchildren, and peers).

4. Specification of instruments or data collection tools. This decision involves the case manager in determining how he or she collects data that are relevant to the concepts being measured. Much has been written about the characteristics of "good instruments" (Mindel, 1985) as well as the use of these instruments in actual human service practice (Jayaratne & Levy, 1979; Bloom & Fischer, 1982; Powers, Meenaghan, & Toomey, 1985). Note closely that the case manager has a range of instruments available including questionnaires, interview tools, client logs, and behavioral observation. In the case of Mrs. Williams, the case manager might employ a social network inventory questionnaire designed to collect data on changes in social network composition and frequency of interaction. The same in-

struments can be employed for both evaluation and for assessment purposes thereby allowing the case manager to gather data regarding client change over time.

5. Specification of the data source.   What is the source of the data collected by the case manager? This question is answered, in part, by the identification of the instrumentation or tools used to capture relevant data. However, the case manager has a range of data sources available that provide some flexibility in selecting the source of the data. Some of these options include the client, significant others, other professionals, client records, and other agency data bases. In some cases the case manager may be concerned about the intrusiveness of data collection. Thus, he or she may rely more on clinical records or another unobtrusive source (Bloom & Fischer, 1985) rather than relying on the client. In the case of evaluating Mrs. Williams's level of social contact the case manager could rely on reports from significant others, a log maintained by the client, or ratings made by the client during an interview with her.

6. Frequency of data collection.   Evaluation data are not necessarily collected only at one point in time. The case manager may want several observation periods so that a client's progress in relationship to a certain goal can be observed over a longitudinal timeline. In the case of Mrs. Williams, the case manager may want to track social contacts over a period of several months in order to determine whether these contacts are changing.

As noted above, these six decisions compose a plan for evaluating the attainment of impact goals. Table 7.3 presents a form which can be used by the case manager in formulating a plan for evaluating the attainment of impact goals.

EVALUATION OF THE GENERAL EFFECTIVENESS OF CASE MANAGEMENT SERVICES

Understanding the general effectiveness of case management lies in evaluating whether case management and the resulting range of services evolving out of this activity contribute to maintaining or enhancing the client's functional status. This assertion is compatible with the assessment and planning frameworks presented within this book. Indeed, the importance of developing a client support network depends on the creation of a structure that will support the client's functioning.

Functional status has been defined in the human services in various ways (Kane, Kane, & Arnold, 1985). In the mental health field considerable effort has been invested in conceptualizing functioning in terms of social role

TABLE 7.3 Planning Format for Evaluating the Attainment of Impact Goals

Statement of Impact Goal	Key Concepts	Indicators	Instruments/ Tools	Data Source	Frequency of Data Collection

performance (Kane et al., 1985; Weissman, 1975; Weissman & Bothwell, 1976). Weissman (1975), as well as many other mental health researchers, has conceptualized social role performance primarily for adults. Potential domains of role performance include work and occupation, leisure, marital relationships, extended family relationships, and civic responsibilities. Because many case managers will work with clients whose social role performance may be limited, this definition may serve as a useful means of evaluating the general effectiveness of case management.

Yet this conceptualization of functioning also presents limitations. Social role performance is weighted heavily in the direction of a normative conception of functioning. That is, people are measured against an implicit or explicit set of standards of normal functioning even though these standards may be ill-defined, or may fail to be sensitive to the client's social situation (Kane et al., 1985).

Functioning—as emphasized in the disability, rehabilitation, and aging literature—is tempered by level of disability, health status, social factors, education, age, and cultural factors. These factors become important for the case manager to consider when conceptualizing and selecting a general measure of a client's functioning.

An alternative way of conceptualizing functioning is through a task-focused means, an approach used widely in the fields of developmental disabilities and aging (Kane et al., 1985). A task-focused conceptualization of functioning addresses a person's performance of self-care activities and instrumental living skills, both of which are influenced by the person's cognitive, behavioral, physical, emotional, and interpersonal capacities. This conceptualization can move case managers away from measuring client functioning against a normative set of standards.

Alternatively, task-focused definitions of functioning are likely to be criterion-oriented. Such definitions assist case managers in thinking about the skills and capacities of their clients in the context of their environments and support systems. Basically, the task-focused approach to functioning inquires into the extent to which a client is developing instrumental skills and capacities which are relevant to self-care.

Systematic evaluation of functioning requires the case manager or the case management agency to select a useful instrument or set of instruments. A careful selection process is very important since the validity, reliability, sensitivity, and feasibility of a particular instrument can be influenced by the characteristics of a client. Again, it is important to highlight the observation that the functional status of a client is influenced by a number of factors.

In situations where the case management agency is serving a fairly homogenous population, the agency may commit itself to one instrument. But in situations where the agency serves different populations, case managers may need a pool of instruments from which they can select ones that address either social role performance or instrumental tasks. Table 7.4 lists examples of instruments that can be employed in the evaluation of client functional status.

Implementing a systematic evaluation of the functional status of the client can begin at the time of assessment. Case managers may select an instrument that serves a dual purpose. One purpose is to employ the instrument as an assessment tool. Here the case manager obtains functional data which can be fed into the case management planning process. Also, the case manager obtains a baseline of the client's functional status against which subsequent observations of the client's functioning can be compared.

EVALUATION OF CLIENT SATISFACTION

Client satisfaction is an important aspect of the evaluation function of case management for several reasons. First, satisfaction represents the individual and personal preferences of the client as they pertain to the implementation and outcome of case management services. Second, by systematically collecting information about these personal preferences the case manager reinforces the role of the client as an active and critical consumer, rather than as a passive recipient of services (Reid & Gundlach, 1983). Related here is a third reason to obtain client satisfaction data. These data serve as an indicator of quality, especially if the items composing a satisfaction questionnaire are designed to elicit information regarding the relevance, value, and worth of the case management services to the client (Poertner, 1985).

Many definitions of satisfaction have been employed within the field of human services. Yet, as discussed by Berger (1983), satisfaction is an affective reaction to services on the part of a recipient. It can be conceptualized, therefore, as a set of either positive or negative feelings the client holds toward the case management services (Berger, 1983).

This definition tends to oversimplify the very complex nature of client satisfaction. In actually operationalizing this concept it is productive to view it as a multidimensional one which may involve such dimensions as:

1. Relevance. That is, the extent to which there is a correspondance between case management services and the client's perception of his or her needs.

TABLE 7.4   Examples of Functioning Instruments for Use in Evaluating
the General Effectiveness of Case Management

---

1. Global Assessment Scale

Developed by Endicott, Spitzer, Fleiss, and Cohen (1976), the Global Assessment Scale focuses on the severity of psychiatric disturbance and limitations such disturbance creates for a person's functioning. Strong emphasis is placed on social functioning as an indicator of positive mental health (Kane et al., 1985).

2. Sickness Impact Profile

Developed by Bergner, Bobbit, Pollard, Martin, and Gilson (1976), and Gilson et al. (1975), this instrument is designed in a true/false format and contains items in 14 functional areas including household management, mobility, emotions, bodily movement, and leisure. The instrument seeks to measure the presence of ill health and related functional limitations, health care needs, and change in health status.

3. Community Adaptation Schedule

Developed by Roen and Burnes (1968), this instrument frequently is used with people coping with psychiatric problems. It is a self-completed assessment tool containing 216 questions. These questions are divided into several categories focusing on community functioning.

4. Health and Daily Living Form

Developed by Moos, Cronkite, Billings, and Finney (1984), this instrument can be completed by a client or administered as an interview. The form is useful in the evaluation of areas such as stress, coping, social functioning, social involvement, and family functioning.

---

2. Impact.   That is, the extent to which the provision of case management services fulfills the client's needs.

3. Gratification.   That is, the extent to which the provision of case management services enhances the client's self-esteem, self-concept, and self-efficacy (Reid & Gundlach, 1983).

4. Characteristics of the Case Manager.   That is, the extent to which the case manager is perceived as being involved with the client and committed to helping him or her.

The four dimensions of relevance, impact, gratification, and characteristics of the case manager provide us with a framework for the design of a client satisfaction instrument. An example of such an instrument is presented in Table 7.5. Note that this exemplar combines both structured and unstructured questions. It is important to pay attention to both types of responses because closed-ended questions may not tap all relevant client feedback. Responses of the client to the open-ended questions and comment sections may reveal valuable data regarding client interaction with administration, with support staff, and with other professionals (Berger, 1983).

In using client satisfaction as an indicator of the outcome of case management services, the case manager must be sensitive to some of the possible methodological problems with this type of measure. There is considerable social pressure on clients to respond to satisfaction questions in positive ways. For example, if the client likes the case manager as a person but disapproves of the services provided, it is likely that the client will still rate the services in a positive way (Berger, 1983).

To counteract these social pressures and to reduce their significance it is important for the case manager and the case management agency to give some forethought to planning the use of satisfaction questionnaires. It is probably wise for the questionnaire to be administered to the client by someone other than the case manager. In addition, it is wise to maintain the client's anonymity so that the confidentiality of client responses is preserved.

Following these procedures will limit the use of satisfaction data with individual clients. Yet, information can be fed back to the case manager through individualized reports masking personal information that might identify a client. In addition, satisfaction data aggregated by program, by department, or by caseload can be fed back to a case manager. What is important here is that case managers receive feedback about the quality of their services as perceived by their clients.

CONCLUSION

Evaluation as conceived in this chapter is a process with multiple foci. As noted at the beginning of the chapter the evaluation of outcome involves the determination of the worth of the case management process itself as reflected in the service support plan, in the attainment of goals, in the general effectiveness of the services, and in client satisfaction.

As with monitoring, the case manager can choose whether the evaluation process will be highly structured and systematic or whether it will be more impressionistic, qualitative, and unstructured. Of course, decisions regarding the formalization of the evaluation process will involve accountability requirements that must be addressed by the case manager according to the time and resources available, and the range of responsibilities included within the case management role. Whichever way the evaluation function is designed, it is critical for the case manager to identify and implement a means for determining the worth of the case management process.

TABLE 7.5 Exemplar Client Satisfaction Questionnaire

We are interested in how you view the case management services you receive from XYZ Agency. Please read each of the statements listed below, and use the following phrases to rate how you feel about the case management services.

6 .... Strongly Agree
5 .... Agree
4 .... Somewhat Agree
3 .... Somewhat Disagree
2 .... Disagree
1 .... Strongly Disagree

_____ 1. I feel the case manager cares about me as a person.
_____ 2. I can count on the case manager explaining things to me carefully.
_____ 3. The services I receive through the case management agency are just what I need.
_____ 4. My outlook about my life has improved since I began using case management services.
_____ 5. I feel the case manager understands a person like me.
_____ 6. I have second thoughts about sending a good friend to this agency for help.
_____ 7. The case manager tries hard to help me meet my needs.
_____ 8. Overall, things have gotten worse for me since I have been using case management services.
_____ 9. If I have problems in the future I will come back to the agency for help.
_____ 10. The case manager is interested in hearing my views on things.
_____ 11. I feel nervous when I go to the case management agency.
_____ 12. I can count on my case manager to help me as much as possible.
_____ 13. My case manager is always available when I need him or her.
_____ 14. In general, the case management services I receive are helping me to be as independent as possible.

Please share with us other comments you may have about the services provided by XYZ Agency:

_____
_____
_____
_____
_____
_____

EXERCISES

1. Select a sample of five or six client records from your current caseload. Systematically review these records evaluating 1) whether the people, services, and other resources identified within the plan are adequate to the attainment of service goals, 2) whether activities and tasks are being implemented appropriately, and 3) whether the service plan remains relevant to client needs.

2. Select one client from the sample selected for Exercise 1. For at least two of the service or impact goals delineated for this client complete the evaluation form displayed in Table 7.3.

3. Reflect on the types of clients served by your agency. List the strengths and limitations of defining client functioning in terms of social role performance. What are the strengths and limitations of defining client functioning using a task-focused or instrumental approach?

4. How can you employ client satisfaction data in your case management practice? List some of the obstacles you will have to overcome in order to implement the use of satisfaction data within your agency.

Chapter 8

Effective Case Management: Guidelines for Practice

KEY QUESTIONS

1. Why will case managers potentially experience conflict in their roles?
2. What are the six precepts of case management practice?
3. Why do case managers maintain a system's perspective? How do you do this in your own work as a case manager?
4. How do you use clinical and administrative skills in your work as a case manager?
5. What are the two dimensions of accountability?
6. Why is integration of services such an important outcome of case management?

INTRODUCTION

Case management is not a panacea for the many ailments of contemporary human services. The problems of fragmentation and discontinuity of service are just two characteristics of our human service delivery systems that reflect the need for mechanisms by which we can achieve a humane and responsive integration of services for people with multiple needs. Certainly there are many mechanisms and strategies for achieving integration of services with case management being just one. Yet case management is unique in our armamentarium since it speaks to organizing and mobilizing often conflicting systems of social supports, social benefits, and social services to meet the needs of individuals who may have neither the power nor the capacities to speak fully for themselves.

Ideally, the key functions of case managers—those of assessment, planning, indirect and direct intervention, monitoring, and evaluation—are the technical means by which case managers seek to meet the needs of their clients. However, case management is not merely a technical enterprise. It is submitted that effective case management requires practitioners to embrace a broad conceptualization of their roles within their respective fields of human service.

This final chapter focuses on articulating this broad conceptualization of case management practice. Six practice concepts are identified. These are designed to summarize the material discussed in previous chapters. Some readers may feel that the guidelines are unrealistic in that they place case managers in conflictual positions or contradictory value situations. By virtue of their roles, case managers are likely to experience substantial conflict in their attempts to reconcile the needs of individual clients with available social resources. This dictum may seem harsh. Nonetheless, case managers need to prepare themselves to experience conflict because it is inherent in the role of effective case management practice.

The second portion of the chapter is devoted to a discussion of the implications of these six concepts for the professional development of case managers. Effective case management practice is learned and developed. It therefore must be groomed on a continuing basis.

SIX PRECEPTS OF CASE MANAGEMENT PRACTICE

1. CASE MANAGERS WORK AT THE "CLIENT LEVEL"

Throughout this book, the case manager has been identified as working with individual clients and as being "client focused." The implication of these phrases is that the case manager is ultimately concerned with the welfare and well-being of his or her individual client. Central to this concern are the broad identification of the client's needs and working with this client in identifying ways to meet these needs.

"Working at the client level" is no easy task. The case manager can be described as a "street level bureaucrat" (Lipsky, 1980); that is, the front line professional who interacts with citizens in the distribution of social benefits. The case manager as street level bureaucrat also holds a position within the organization and may experience a strain between representing the interests of the client and representing those of the organization (Dill, 1987). Awareness of this ongoing dilemma must be in the forefront of the case manager's mind. Promoting client autonomy, functioning, and self-direction may not be possible if case managers conceive of themselves primarily as representatives of the interests of their sponsoring organizations. If this is the situation, case managers must recognize that they cannot fully embrace the role of client representative. A response to this constraint would be for the case manager to identify an external advocate who could work with the client and the case manager to serve as a check on bureaucratic interests.

2. CASE MANAGERS MAINTAIN A SYSTEM'S PERSPECTIVE

"Systemic" should be a key word in the vocabulary of case managers. This word basically means that case managers view the client and the needs of the client within a holistic framework of interacting parts. The case manager has an appreciation for the effects of the environment on the client, and the effects of the client on the environment. The systemic concern of the case manager, however, is whether clients can meet their needs through the systems in which they are embedded.

Thus, the case manager brings together a concern for the needs of the client, and for the capacities of the client and the system to meet these needs. This system was articulated as having two major dimensions for the purpose of effective case management practice. The so-called informal system invokes the functioning of primary groups in meeting client needs. Formal systems of social and human services also provide resources in meeting client needs.

Given the systemic nature of their work, case managers may be engaged in a balancing act. Since the goals of case management practice are to promote client autonomy, functioning, and self-direction, the case manager must be attuned to assuring that client self-care capacities are never compromised by mobilizing either formal or informal resources to meet client needs. This balancing act requires case managers to engage in a vigilant monitoring process to assure that their clients always have opportunities to use their personal resources in meeting their needs while being ready to mobilize and engage other resources if needed by clients.

3. CASE MANAGERS USE ADMINISTRATIVE PROCESSES AND SKILLS

From my perspective case managers serve as administrators, and must take seriously their roles as managers. Reflection on the content of previous chapters will underscore the critical administrative roles and tasks of case managers including:

Organizing and leading teams of professionals in case decision-making.
Planning the delivery of client services.
Working with the client and other professionals in setting and monitoring objectives.
Monitoring the completion of tasks and responsibilities on part of the client, social network members, and human service professionals.
Providing feedback to individuals involved in the delivery of support and services regarding the effectiveness of their efforts.

4. CASE MANAGERS USE CLINICAL PROCESSES AND SKILLS

Ignoring the clinical and interpersonal practice dimensions of case management is counterproductive. A salient debate in the field of case management, especially within the mental health arena, centers on whether case managers should be involved clinically with their clients or should focus mainly on activities involving organizing client services.

The model I presented in this book prescribes an integration of direct and indirect services. Interpersonal practice, from my perspective, is just as important a function of case managers as the administrative and management functions. First of all, underlying effective case management practice is a caring and individualized relationship between client and case manager. Second, case managers must be skilled in interpersonal practice since they will use these skills in conducting individualized assessments of client needs. Case managers must also be knowledgeable of the clinical expertise of other disciplines and must use this knowledge in identifying the need to conduct specialized assessments, as well as in evaluating the quality of these assessments.

Finally, it is likely that case managers will work with their clients on an individual basis. Helping clients to develop their skills, working with clients in the assessment and planning processes, and perhaps even intervening in crises all require interpersonal practice skills on part of the case manager.

5. CASE MANAGERS SERVE AS SOURCES OF ACCOUNTABILITY

Case managers occupy central positions within complex information and service delivery networks. Given such positions, and the central roles of case managers, they are likely to become accountable for client service delivery. "Accountability" means that the case manager has sufficient knowledge and information about the client so that he or she is responsible for identifying problems or unfulfilled needs that the client is experiencing, and for assuring that the client's current plan and array of services respond to these problems or needs.

There are many forms of accountability. My scheme breaks accountability down into two dimensions:

(1) Effort-Oriented Accountability. In this type of accountability the case manager assures that the responsibilities, activities, and tasks of key actors making up the client support network are being implemented according to the client service and support plan. The major focus of the case manager is assuring that the plan as conceptualized and designed is being appropriately implemented by the key actors identified within it. Effort-oriented accountability requires the case manager to engage in effective monitoring.

(2) Effectiveness-Oriented Accountability. In this type of accountability the case manager assures that the plan as conceived and implemented is an effective one. That is, the implementation of the plan results in meeting and fulfilling the identified needs of the client.

Accountability should be a dynamic concept. It feeds into the need of case managers to achieve cross-sectional and longitudinal continuity of care. An accountable case manager is not only able to muster the necessary resources to address the client's needs at any one time, but is also able to change and modify these resources as the client's needs change over time.

6. CASE MANAGERS ATTEMPT TO ACHIEVE INTEGRATION
OF SERVICE DELIVERY

One of the primary evaluative criteria of the effectiveness of case management is whether the needs of clients can be achieved in an integrated manner. "Integration," as articulated in Chapter 1, means that client services and supports are provided in a complementary manner and ultimately make

TABLE 8.1 Professional Development Scheme

Foci of Professional Development	Client-Level Practice	Systems Perspective	Administrative Processes	Clinical Processes	Accountability	Service Integration
			Areas of Professional Development			
Enhancement of knowledge	Understanding how social and psychological factors influence needs	Understanding social policy systems and related social benefits	Understanding how work groups behave and develop	Understanding basic problem-solving processes	Understanding various meanings and definitions of accountability	Understanding problems and difficulties inherent in achieving interagency and interdisciplinary cooperation and coordination
	Understanding the relationship of culture, race, and ethnicity to needs	Understanding social support systems	Understanding leadership and membership roles	Understanding disability and its relationship to social functioning	Understanding evaluative mechanisms for achieving effort-oriented accountability	Understanding the communication and information processing requirements of effective teamwork
	Understanding risk and vulnerability of client	Understanding how needs can be met through formal and informal support systems	Understanding the functions of planning, monitoring, and evaluation	Understanding roles, functions and expertise of major human services disciplines	Understanding evaluative mechanisms for achieving effectiveness-oriented accountability	Understanding the planning process so that compatible goals and objectives are developed
Enhancement of skills	Communication and relationship building skills	Identifying relevant social benefits	Building and maintaining effective teams	Assessing needs and problems of clients	Developing client support and service plans that can support accountability	Gaining cooperation and collaboration of team members

Identifying and integrating diverse services and activities that address a unified set of goals	Writing reports that reflect accountability of self and other professionals	Interviewing and communicating with person who presents functional limitations	Working in an interdisciplinary environment	Gaining involvement of social network members	Translating needs into prescriptive action strategies
Monitoring and evaluating level of integration of services	Collecting and managing data and information for accountability	Helping person clarify his needs, preferences, and desires	Managing data and information within case management process		Skills in involving clients in decision making
Awareness of oneself as a boundary spanner	Awareness of one's dual role of being accountable and holding others accountable	Awareness of one's strengths and limitations as a clinician	Awareness of one's leadership style	Awareness of how one uses systems perspective	**Enhancement of self-awareness** — Awareness of one's strengths and weaknesses in working with clients
Awareness of the possibility of role strain	Awareness that accountability process can create conflict	Awareness of one's communication and interpersonal styles	Awareness of one's communication and interpersonal styles	Awareness of one's approach to defining client problems	Awareness of one's attitudes toward clients
Awareness of communication, interpersonal, and information processing capacities					

a contribution to the development and enhancement of client autonomy, functioning, and self-direction.

Although conceptually abstract, achievement of integration requires that the services and supports that are organized and implemented do not work at cross-purposes. For example, the case manager must assure that the formal human services designed to respond to a client's needs do not reduce his capacity to care for himself, or for his social network to respond effectively to his needs.

A NOTE ON PROFESSIONAL DEVELOPMENT

The framework of case management presented in this book presents many challenges for the professional development of case managers. The author would underscore the importance of professional development because this is a primary means by which case managers will gain the skills and capacities to engage in more effective practice. Certainly case managers will benefit from their own disciplinary training and the acquisition of undergraduate and graduate education in the human services. Yet, the roles and functions of case managers are unique enough to demand on-going exposure of practitioners to new knowledge, new skills, and new capacities while on the job.

I have combined into Table 8.1 the six practice precepts presented above with three substantive areas of professional development. This table presents a "Scheme of Professional Development" for case managers by identifying examples of knowledge, skill, and self-awareness capacities that can be developed by case managers. It is suggested that the reader reflect on the model presented in the book and on the practice precepts presented above. After examining the examples of knowledge, skill, and self-awareness capacities presented in Table 8.1, readers can outline their own plans for professional development.

CONCLUSION

This chapter concludes my exploration of case management and its role in the human services. This area of human service practice is challenging, and can hold many rewards for professionals who commit themselves to the enterprise of effectively fulfilling the needs of people through the identification and mobilization of societal resources and social supports.

As emphasized in different parts of this book, case management is not an easy task. By virtue of its complexity, case management can create stress, strain, and conflict for practitioners. Yet if case managers are committed to identifying and fulfilling client needs, and to dealing with systems that may be reluctant to serve and support a person, then conflict will be inherent in the roles of case managers. Perhaps by viewing conflict as a normative and expected characteristic of case management practice it might become easier to manage both for a client and for oneself.

In closing, the author wishes his readers success as they prepare for practice as case managers or continue their professional work. It is hoped that this guide will assist readers in reflecting on their own approach to case management practice.

REFERENCES

Aiken, M., Dewar, R., DiTomaso, N., Hage, J., & Zeitz, G. (1975). *Coordinating human services*. San Francisco: Jossey-Bass.

Albert, D. H. (1985). *People power: Applying nonviolence theory*. Philadelphia: New Society Publishers.

Apolloni, T., & Cooke, T. P. (1984). *A new look at guardianship: Protective services that support personalized living*. Baltimore: Paul H. Brookes.

Auvine, B., Densmore, B., Extrom, M., Poole, S., & Shanklin, M. (1978). *A manual for group facilitators*. Madison, WI: Center for Conflict Resolution.

Avery, M., Auvine, B., Streibel, B., & Weiss, L. (1981). *Building united judgment: A handbook for consensus decision making*. Madison, WI: Center for Conflict Resolution.

Baker, F. (1977). The interface between professional and natural support systems. *Clinical Social Work Journal, 5*(2), 139-148.

Barten, H. (1971). The expanding spectrum of the brief therapies. In H. Barten (Ed.). *Brief therapies* (pp. 3-27). New York: Behavioral Publications.

Bellack, A. S., & Hersen, M. (1979). *Research and practice in social skills training*. New York: Plenum.

Berger, M. (1983). Toward maximizing the utility of consumer satisfaction as an outcome. In M. J. Lambert, E. R. Christensen, & S. S. DeJulio (Eds.). *The assessment of psychotherapy outcome*. New York: John Wiley.

Bergner, M., Bobbitt, R. A., Pollard, W. E., Martin, D. P., & Gilson, B. (1976). Sickness impact profile: Validation of a health status measure. *International Journal of Health Services, 6*, 393-415.

Blake, R., Mouton, J., & Allen, R. (1987). *Spectacular teamwork: How to develop the leadership skills for team success*. New York: John Wiley.

Bloom, B. (1981). *Primary prevention*. Englewood Cliffs, NJ: Prentice-Hall.

Bloom, M., & Fischer, J. (1982). *Evaluating practice: Guidelines for the accountable professional*. Englewood-Cliffs, NJ: Prentice-Hall.

Boissevain, J. (1974). *Friends of friends*. Oxford, England: Blackwell.

Bradford, L. P. (1976). *Making meetings work: A guide for leaders and group members*. San Diego: University Associates.

Brill, N. (1976). *Teamwork: Working together in the human services*. New York: Lippincott.

Bronfenbrenner, U. (1979). *The ecology of human development*. Cambridge, MA: Harvard University Press.

Caplan, G. (1974). *Support systems and community mental health*. New York: Behavioral Publications.

Cohen, M., Vitalo, R., Anthony, W., & Pierce, R. (1980). *The skills of community service coordination*. Psychiatric rehabilitation practice series (Book 6). Baltimore: University Park Press.

Compton, B. R., & Galaway, B. (1979). *Social work processes*. Homewood, IL: Dorsey Press.

Coulton, C. (1979). *Social work quality assurance programs: A comparative analysis.* Washington, DC: NASW.

Curtis, W. R. (1973). Community human service networks: New roles for mental health workers. *Psychiatric Annals, 3*(7), 23-42.

Curtis, W. R. (1974). Team problem solving in a social network. *Psychiatric Annals, 3*(7), 11-27.

Curtis, W. R. (1979). *The future use of social networks in mental health.* Boston: Social Matrix.

Deitchman, W. S. (1980). How many case managers does it take to screw in a light bulb? *Hospital and Community Psychiatry, 31* (11), 788-789.

Delbecq, A. L., Van de Ven, A. H., & Gustafson, D. H. (1975). *Group techniques for program planning: A guide to nominal group and delphi processes.* Glenview, IL: Scott, Foresman.

Dill, A. (1987). Issues in case management for the chronically mentally ill. In D. Mechanic (Ed.). *Improving mental health services: What the social sciences can tell us* (pp. 61-70). San Francisco: Jossey-Bass.

Dixon, S. L. (1979). *Working with people in crisis: Theory and practice.* St. Louis: C. V. Mosby.

Donovan, J. (1984, Winter). Team nurse and social worker: Avoiding role conflict. *The Journal of Hospice Care,* 21-23.

Ducanis, A. J., & Golin, A. K. (1979). *The interdisciplinary health care team.* Germantown, MD: Aspen.

Egan, G. (1985). *Change agent skills in helping and human service settings.* Monterey, CA: Brooks/Cole.

Endicott, J., Spitzer, R., Fleiss, J., & Cohen, J. (1976). The global assessment scale: A procedure for measuring overall severity of psychiatric disturbance. *Archives of General Psychiatry, 33,* 766-771.

Epstein, I., & Tripodi, T. (1977). *Research techniques for program planning, monitoring, and evaluation.* New York: Columbia University Press.

Erickson, G. D. (1975). The concept of personal network in clinical practice. *Family Process, 14,* 487-498.

Falloon, I., Boyd, J. L., & McGill, C. W. (1984). *Family care of schizophrenia.* New York: Guilford.

Fox, W. (1987). *Effective group problem-solving.* San Francisco: Jossey-Bass.

Gallessich, J. (1982). *The profession and practice of consultation.* San Francisco: Jossey-Bass.

Gardner, J. F. (1980). Interdisciplinary team process and individualized program planning. In J. Gardner, L. Long, R. Nichols, and D. Iagulli (Eds.). *Program issues in developmental disabilities: A resource manual for surveyors and reviewers.* Baltimore: Paul H. Brookes.

Gates, B. L. (1980). *Social program administration: The implementation of social policy.* Englewood Cliffs, NJ: Prentice-Hall.

Germain, C. B., & Gitterman, A. (1980). *The life model of social work practice.* New York: Columbia University Press.

Gil, D. (1976a). *Unravelling social policy.* Cambridge, MA: Schenkman.

Gil, D. (1976b). *The challenge of social equality.* Cambridge, MA: Schenkman.

Gilbert, N., & Specht, H. (1974). *Dimensions of social welfare policy.* Englewood Cliffs, NJ: Prentice-Hall.

Gilbert, N., & Specht, H. (Eds.). (1981). *Handbook of the social services.* Englewood Cliffs, NJ: Prentice-Hall.

Gilson, B. S., Gilson, J. S., Bergner, M., Bobbitt, R. A., Kressel, S., Pollard, W., & Vesselago, M. (1975). The sickness impact profile: Development of an outcome measure of health care. *American Journal of Public Health, 65*, 1304-1310.

Goldstein, A. (1981). *Psychological skill training: The structured learning technique.* New York: Pergamon.

Goldstein, A., Sprafkin, R., Gershaw, N., & Klein, P. (1980). *Skill-streaming the adolescent: A structured learning approach to teaching prosocial skills.* Champaign, IL: Research Press.

Goldstein, H. (1981). Generalist social work practice. In N. Gilbert & H. Specht (Eds.). *Handbook of the social services.* Englewood-Cliffs, NJ: Prentice-Hall.

Gottlieb, B. H., & Schroter, C. (1978). Collaboration and resource exchange between professionals and natural support systems. *Professional Psychology, 9*, 614-621.

Grinnell, R. M., Kyte, N. S., & Bostwick, G. J. (1981). Environmental modification. In A. Maluccio (Ed.). *Promoting competence in clients.* New York: Free Press.

Halpern, A., & Fuhrer, M. (Eds.). (1984). *Functional assessment in rehabilitation.* Baltimore: Paul H. Brookes.

Halpern, A., Lehman, J., Irvin, L., & Heiry, T. (1982). *Contemporary assessment for mentally retarded adolescents and adults.* Baltimore: University Park Press.

Hasenfeld, Y. (1983). *Human service organizations.* Englewood Cliffs, NJ: Prentice-Hall.

Havelock, R. G. (1973). *The change agent's guide to innovation in education.* Englewood Cliffs, NJ: Educational Technology Publications.

Hepworth, D. H., & Larsen, J. (1982). *Direct social work practice: Theory and skills.* Homewood, IL: Dorsey.

Herzog, K. (1985). Documentation of hospice care plan development and team meetings. *Quality Review Bulletin*, 190-192.

Jayaratne, S., & Levy, R. L. (1979). *Empirical clinical practice.* New York: Columbia University Press.

Johnson, P. J., & Rubin, A. (1983). Case management in mental health: A social work domain? *Social Work, 28*(1), 49-56.

Kane, R. A., Kane, R. L., & Arnold, S. (1985). *Measuring social functioning in mental health studies: Concepts and instruments.* Washington, DC: USGPO.

Kanter, J. S. (1985). Case management of the young adult chronic patient: A clinical perspective. In J. S. Kanter (Ed.). *Clinical issues in treating the chronic mentally ill.* San Francisco: Jossey-Bass.

Kapferer, B. (1969). Norms and manipulation of relationships in a work context. In J. Clyde Mitchell (Ed.). *Social networks in urban situations.* Manchester, England: Manchester University Press.

King, J. A., Morris, L., & Fitz-Gibbon, C. (1987). *How to assess program implementation.* Newbury Park, CA: Sage.

Kokopeli, B., & Lakey, G. (n.d.). *Leadership for change: Toward a feminist model.* Philadelphia: New Society Publishers.

Lamb, H. R. (1980). Therapist-case managers: More than brokers of services. *Hospital and Community Psychiatry, 31*(11), 762-764.

Lawrence, M. A. (1975). *Developing program models for the human services.* New York: Behavioral Publications.

Lenrow, P. B., & Burch, R. W. (1981). Mutual aid and professional services: Opposing or complementary? In B. H. Gottlieb (Ed.). *Social networks and social support.* Beverly Hills, CA: Sage.

Levine, I., & Fleming, M. (n.d.). *Human resource development: Issues in case management.*

Washington, DC: National Institute of Mental Health.

Lipsky, M. (1980). *Street-level bureaucracy: Dilemmas of the individual in public services.* New York: Russell Sage.

Llamas, R. (1976). *An exploratory and comparative study of the psychosocial networks of a group of normals and a group of personality disorders.* Unpublished doctoral dissertation, U. S. International University.

Maguire, L. (1983). *Understanding social networks.* Beverly Hills, CA: Sage.

Maluccio, A. N. (Ed.) (1981). *Promoting competence in clients.* New York: Free Press.

McKillip, J. (1987). *Need analysis: Tools for human services and education.* Beverly Hills, CA: Sage.

Mindel, C. H. (1985). Instrument design. In R. M. Grinnell (Ed). *Social work research and evaluation.* (2nd ed.). Itasca, IL: F. E. Peacock.

Mitchell, J. C. (1969). The concept and use of social networks. In J. C. Mitchell (Ed.). *Social networks in urban situations.* Manchester, England: University of Manchester Press.

Mitchell, R. E., & Trickett, E. (1980). Social network research and psychosocial adaptation: Implications for mental health practice. In P. Insel (Ed.). *Environmental variables and the prevention of mental illness.* Toronto: Lexington Books.

Mizrahi, T., & Abramson, J. (1985). Sources of strain between physicians and social workers: Implications for social workers in health care settings. *Social Work in Health Care, 10* (3), 33-51.

Moore, C. M. (1987). *Group techniques for idea building.* Newbury Park, CA: Sage.

Moos, R. H., Cronkite, R. C., Billings, A. G., & Finney, J. (1984). *Health and daily living form manual.* Palo Alto, CA: Social Ecology Laboratory, Stanford University.

Morris, L., & Fitz-Gibbon, C. (1978a). *How to deal with goals and objectives.* Beverly Hills, CA: Sage.

Morris, L., & Fitz-Gibbon, C. (1978b). *How to measure program implementation.* Beverly Hills, CA: Sage.

Morris, L., & Fitz-Gibbon, C. (1978c). *How to measure achievement.* Beverly Hills, CA: Sage.

Morris, L., Fitz-Gibbon, C., & Lindheim, E. (1987). *How to measure performance and use tests.* Beverly Hills, CA: Sage.

Moxley, D. (1983). *Assessment of the social support networks of persons who have major psychiatric disorders: Development and investigation of an applied clinical instrument.* Unpublished doctoral dissertation, Ohio State University.

Moxley, D. (1984). *Crisis and outreach as case management functions.* Paper presented at the Conference on Case Management: Putting the Pieces Together. Office of Program Evaluation and Research. Ohio Department of Mental Health. Toledo, OH.

Moxley, D. (1988a). Measuring the social support networks of persons with major psychiatric disorders: A pilot investigation. *Psychosocial Rehabilitation Journal, 11*(3), 19-27.

Moxley, D. (1988b). Exploring the validity of social network indicators for use in psychosocial rehabilitation. *Psychosocial Rehabilitation Journal 11*(4), 3-10.

Moxley, D., Raider, M., & Cohen, S. (1987). *Facilitating family involvement in services to developmentally disabled persons.* Unpublished manuscript.

National Institute of Handicapped Research. (1985). Self-determination among people with disabilities. *Rehab Brief, 8*(5), pp. 1-4.

National Institute of Mental Health. (1977). *Guidelines for program evaluation.* (Working draft). Rockville, MD: Author.

O'Neill, M. J. (1984). *The general method of social work practice.* Englewood Cliffs, NJ: Prentice-Hall.

O'Neill, P., & Trickett, E. J. (1982). *Community consultation.* San Francisco: Jossey-Bass.

154 THE PRACTICE OF CASE MANAGEMENT

Parsons, R. D., & Meyers, J. (1984). *Developing consultation skills.* San Francisco: Jossey-Bass.

Patton, M. Q. (1987). *How to use qualitative methods in evaluation.* Newbury Park, CA: Sage.

Pierce, D. (1984). *Policy for the social work practitioner.* New York: Longman.

Poertner, J. (1985). A scale for measuring clients' satisfaction with parent education. *Social work research and abstracts, 21*(3), 23-28.

Powers, G. T., Meenaghan, T. M., & Toomey, B. G. (1985). *Practice-focused research: Integrating human service practice and research.* Englewood Cliffs, NJ: Prentice-Hall.

Quinn, J., Segal, J., Raisz, H., & Johnson, C. (Eds.). (1982). *Coordinating community services for the elderly.* New York: Springer.

Reid, P., & Gundlach, J. H. (1983). A scale for the measurement of consumer satisfaction with social services. *Journal of Social Service Research, 7*(1), 37-53.

Roberts-DeGennaro, M. (1987). Developing case management as a practice model. *Social Casework, 68*(8), 466-470.

Roen, S. R., & Burnes, A. J. (1968). *Community adaptation schedule: Preliminary manual.* New York: Behavioral Publications.

Roessler, R. T., & Rubin, S. E. (1982). *Case management and rehabilitation counseling.* Baltimore: University Park Press.

Rosenfeld, J. (1983). The domain and expertise of social work: A conceptualization. *Social Work, 28,* 186-191.

Rossi, R. J., Gilmartin, K. J., & Dayton, C. W. (1982). *Agencies working together: A guide to coordination and planning.* Beverly Hills, CA: Sage.

Rothman, J., Erlich, J. L., & Teresa, J. G. (1981). *Changing organizations and community programs.* Beverly Hills, CA: Sage.

Rutman, L. (1984). Evaluability assessment. In L. Rutman (Ed.). *Evaluation research methods: A basic guide.* Beverly Hills, CA: Sage.

Sampson, E., & Marthas, M. (1977). *Group process for the health professions.* New York: Wiley.

Sanborn, C. J. (Ed.). (1983). *Case management in mental health services.* New York: Haworth.

Schaefer, M. (1987). *Implementing change in service programs: Project planning and management.* Beverly Hills, CA: Sage.

Schutz, R. P., Vogelsberg, R., & Rusch, F. R. (1980). A behavioral approach to integrating individuals into the community. In A. R. Novak & L. W. Heal (Eds.). *Integration of developmentally disabled individuals into the community* (pp. 107-120). Baltimore: Paul H. Brookes.

Seaman, D. (1981). *Working effectively with task-oriented groups.* New York: McGraw-Hill.

Seligman, M. (1975). *Helplessness: On depression, development, and death.* New York: Freeman.

Siporin, M. (1975). *Introduction to social work practice.* New York: Macmillan.

Sorenson, J., Hammer, R., & Windle, C. (1979). The four A's—Acceptability, availability, accessibility, awareness. In G. Landsberg, W. Neigher, R. Hammer, C. Windle, & J. Woy (Eds.). *Evaluation in practice.* Rockville, MD: NIMH.

Sosin, M., & Caulum, S. (1983). Advocacy: A conceptualization for social work practice. *Social Work, 28*(1), 12-17.

Springer, D., & Brubaker, T. H. (1984). *Family caregivers and dependent elderly.* Beverly Hills, CA: Sage.

Stech, E., & Ratliffe, S. (1985). *Effective group communication: How to get action by working in groups.* Lincolnwood, IL: National Textbook.

Steinberg, R. M., & Carter, G. W. (1983). *Case management and the elderly*. Lexington, MA: Lexington Books.

Stufflebeam, D., & Shinkfield, A. (1986). *Systematic evaluation*. Boston: Kluwer, Nijhoff.

Sundel, R., & Sundel, S. S. (1975). *Behavior modification in the human services*. New York: John Wiley.

Test, M. (1979). Continuity of care in community treatment. In L. Stein (Ed.). *Community support systems for the long term patient*. San Francisco: Jossey-Bass.

Thomas, E. J. (1984). *Designing interventions for the helping professions*. Beverly Hills, CA: Sage.

Tolsdorf, C. (1976). Social networks, support, and coping: An exploratory study. *Family Process, 15*(4), 407-417.

Tropman, J. E. (1980). *Effective meetings: Improving group decision-making*. Beverly Hills, CA: Sage.

Weiss, R. S. (1969). The fund of sociability. *Transaction, 6*(9), 36-43.

Weiss, R. S. (1974). The provisions of social relationships. In Z. Rubin (Ed.). *Doing unto others*. Engelwood Cliffs, NJ: Prentice-Hall.

Weissman, A. (1976). Industrial social services: Linkage technology. *Social Casework, 57*, 50-54.

Weissman, M. (1975). The assessment of social adjustment: A review of techniques. *Archives of General Psychiatry, 32*, 357-375.

Weissman, M., & Bothwell, S. (1976). The assessment of social adjustment by patient self-report. *Archives of General Psychiatry, 33*, 1111-1115.

Wellman, B. (1979). The community question: The intimate networks of East Yorkers. *American Journal of Sociology, 84*, 1201-1231.

Whittaker, J. K., & Garbarino, J. (Eds.) (1983). *Social support networks: Informal helping in the human services*. New York: Aldine.

Whittaker, J. K., Schinke, S. P., & Gilchrist, L. D. (1986). The ecological paradigm in child, youth, and family services: Implications for policy and practice. *Social Service Review, 60*(4), 483-503.

Wolfensberger, W., & Zauha, H. (Eds.). (1973). *Citizen advocacy and protective services for the impaired and handicapped*. Toronto: National Institute on Mental Retardation.

Zald, M. (1979). Organizations as polities: An analysis of community organization agencies. In F. M. Cox, J. L. Erlich, J. Rothman, & J. E. Tropman (Eds.). *Strategies of community organization* (3rd ed.). Itasca, IL: F. E. Peacock.

Zawadaski, R. T. (Ed.). (1984). *Community-based systems of long term care*. New York: Haworth.

About the Author

DAVID P. MOXLEY, Ph.D., is Assistant Professor in the Wayne State University School of Social Work, Detroit, Michigan. His experience in the human services field includes clinical practice, administration, research and evaluation, and consultation. During the 1988-89 academic year Dr. Moxley was a National Institute of Mental Health Fellow at the University of Michigan School of Social Work. The author's direct practice experience with case management, his consultation activities, and his teaching of social work methods have provided material for this volume.

NOTES

NOTES

NOTES